★ ★ GEORGE GERSHWIN ★ ★

MAN AND LEGEND

By MERLE

Georgeman

With a Note on the Author by

JOHN
CHARLES
THOMAS

New York

DUELL, SLOAN AND PEARCE

ARMITAGE

Gershwin

and legend

To Isabelle

Contents

A Note on the Author *by John Charles Thomas*   7

My Brother *by Ira Gershwin*   11

1. The Nature of George Gershwin   21

2. Discoveries and Inventions   39

3. The Man   60

4. The Critics   84

5. George Gershwin, as the Legend Grew   122

6. *Porgy and Bess*   130

7. Gershwin's Contemporaries   139

8. The History of *Porgy and Bess*   147

Bibliography and Acknowledgments   179

George Gershwin's Concert Works   181

George Gershwin's Music in Stage Productions   182

George Gershwin's Motion-Picture Scores   183

Motion Pictures Adapted from Gershwin Musicals   183

George Gershwin's Great Songs, and the Artists Who Introduced Them   184

A Gershwin Discography   186

A Note on the Author

BY JOHN CHARLES THOMAS

COLUMBUS discovered America, they say. Merle Armitage, a few centuries later, discovered the essence of this state of mind we call the United States. After hearing of the accomplishments of this inspired impresario, who helped pilot to fame Rosa Ponselle, Galli-Curci, Martha Graham, and many others; who published the first books on Stravinsky, Schoenberg, Edward Weston, Paul Klee; and whose success as a cook was awarded the coveted *Cordon Bleu* of the International Wine and Food Society, a recital which closed with a description of his celebrated *Fit for a King*, a charmingly innocent woman sought him out to ask: "How do you know when someone or something is going to be great?"

Merle asked for an egg.

"How do you know when an egg will produce a chicken? You look through it in the light."

Merle Armitage has always possessed this particular power.

He has had remarkable success "looking through" persons and recognizing their potentialities. His primary enthusiasms are seldom misplaced. He has relied on his intuition, plus an enormous culture and his knowledge of human beings. From the candidates, he has always screened out the best.

A bird's-eye view of his career is illuminating.

As a very young civil engineer, he damaged his eyes working in the near-tropical sun, and at the drafting board by night. He was forced to abandon that profession. At eighteen, his new concepts of theater staging were published in *Cosmopolitan* magazine, and this brought him the opportunity to join the staff of one of the chief American impresarios.

When most men of his age were in universities, he was managing the concerts of John McCormack, Mary Garden, Galli-Curci, Alma Gluck, Mischa Elman, Paderewski, Gieseking, and other stars. He organized national tours for Pavlowa and her ballet, the Scotti Opera Company with Geraldine Farrar, and was one of the executives of the Diaghileff Ballet Russe. He was the first to take Martha Graham on a transcontinental tour.

In the midst of all these peripatetic responsibilities he gathered and acquired an outstanding collection of modern art, and built a library of more than three thousand books.

In 1932, not completely submerged by his other activities, he commenced the writing and designing of books. They were unique in two respects. They introduced in their texts artists and musicians then unknown, while in design they attempted a visual counterpart of the text. In both text and design he ranged far and wide, and now more than ninety-five Merle Armitage books include volumes on railroading, the navy, and on design itself. He has been president of the American Institute of Graphic Arts. For his unique contribution in the making of books he received the Gold Medal from the American Institute of Architects.

World War II found him completing his work as one of the founders of opera on the Pacific Coast. Commissioned a major in the Army Air Force, he was attached to the Matériel Command at Wright Field. There he became an impresario to a group of distinguished engineers, developing new sources of supply for intensive production of airplanes. Later in the war, he and six other officers were assigned the task of forming the rotation system for men in combat. After four years, he terminated his service as a colonel with the Legion of Merit.

After the war, he joined the art department at MGM as assistant to Cedric Gibbons. Gardner Cowles then selected him for the team that was to reconstruct *Look* magazine, and he became a member of the editorial board and art director of that magazine. He became a pioneer in photo-journalism and the new communicative type of layout as applied to magazines.

Merle Armitage, the impresario, the book designer, the writer, the leading man in the field of modern art, is also the man who knows America best, and the best of America. He has always sensed the potentials of this boiling caldron, with its limitless future.

It was he who managed George Gershwin's final concerts and became his close friend. He was the first to produce *Porgy and Bess* following the death of George. His years of association with composers and performers, his friendships with Stravinsky, Varèse, Schoenberg, and other giants of our time give him the frame of reference to place George Gershwin in his proper place as our greatest American composer.

Past associations with Merle Armitage have always been pleasant and very fruitful, and I earnestly commend him and his book to your thoughtful attention.

JOHN CHARLES THOMAS

My Brother

BY IRA GERSHWIN

MY BROTHER, born in Brooklyn, New York, September 26, 1898, was the second of four children of Morris and Rose Bruskin Gershwin. I was the oldest, then came George, then Arthur, and last, our sister Frances. Most of our early boyhood was spent on the lower East Side of Manhattan where my father engaged in various activities: restaurants, Russian and Turkish baths, bakeries, a cigar store and pool parlor on the Forty-second Street side of what is now Grand Central Station, bookmaking at the Brighton Beach Race Track for three exciting but disastrous weeks. We were always moving. When my father sold a business and started another we would inevitably move to the new neighborhood. George and I once counted more than twenty-five different flats and apartments we remembered having lived in during those days.

It was when we were living on Second Avenue that my mother added a piano to our home. George was about twelve at this time. No sooner had the upright been lifted through the window to the "front-room" floor than George sat down and played a popular tune of the day. I remember being particularly impressed by his left hand. I had had no idea he could play and found out that despite his roller-skating activities, the kid parties he attended, the many street games he participated in (with an occasional resultant bloody nose), he had found time to experiment on a player piano at the home of a friend on Seventh Street. Although our piano was purchased with my taking lessons in mind, it was decided that George might prove the brighter pupil.

His first teacher was a Miss Green. She was succeeded by a Hungarian band leader, impressively mustached, who was down on his uppers and condescended to take an occasional pupil. He was the composer of a "Theodore Roosevelt March," and his fancy ran to band and orchestra literature. George was studying a piano version of the "William Tell Overture" when he was brought to Charles Hambitzer, a talented pianist and composer of light music. Hambitzer, quick to recognize his ability, encouraged his harmonies and introduced him to the works of the masters, with special emphasis on Chopin and Debussy. George attended the High School of Commerce for a short period. During that time he was pianist for the morning-assembly exercises.

At the age of fifteen and for a consideration of fifteen dollars a week George became a pianist in the "professional department" of Jerome H. Remick and Company, publishers of popular music. He was probably the youngest piano pounder ever employed in Tin Pan Alley. He played all day, traveled to nearby cities to accompany the song pluggers, was sent to vaudeville houses to report which acts were using Remick songs, wrote a tune now and then, and, whenever he could, attended concerts. Several of his confrères looked askance at this side of his activities. A song plugger was quite indignant: "I went to a recital once. What's the idea? Why, they only had a piano on the stage."

One day George submitted a song of his own to the professional manager. He was told: "You're here as a pianist, not a writer. We've got plenty of writers under contract." Shortly after he gave up his job. Soon, at another house, a song of his was accepted. This was in 1916 and the song was called "When You Want 'Em You Can't Get 'Em, When You've Got 'Em You Don't Want 'Em." George received an advance of five dollars. Murray Roth, who wrote the lyrics, was more persuasive and received fifteen. The next published song, written with Sigmund Romberg and Harold Atteridge, was sung in *The Passing Show of 1916*. This also had an arresting title— "Making of a Girl"—and proved pretty conclusively that a girlie's looks were greatly dependent on her wearing the proper clothes. As the returns on this song were somewhat less than seven dollars George decided he couldn't live on royalties.

At this stage he became rehearsal pianist for the Dillingham-Ziegfeld production of *Miss 1917*. During a Sunday-night "concert" at the Century Theatre where *Miss 1917* was playing, Miss Vivienne Segal introduced two of his numbers. These brought him to the attention of Max Dreyfus, then head of Harms, Incorporated, music publishers. He signed with Dreyfus at thirty-five dollars a week. Although he had many more financially flattering offers he decided that his place was with Dreyfus, who was not only a publisher of musical comedies and operettas but also a fine musician and student of the classics. During this time George continued his studies with Edward Kilenyi and then Rubin Goldmark. There was rarely a period in his life when he was not studying. His last teacher was Dr. Joseph Shillinger. I find among the notes of his lessons with Shillinger strange graphs with headings such as "Rhythmic Groups Resulting from the Interference of Several Synchronized Periodicities" and "Groups with the Fractioning Around the Axis of Symmetry."

George began interpolating in various shows. His lyrics were mostly by Irving Caesar. He also began to accept lyrics by Arthur Francis (a pseudonym I concocted from the names of my other brother and my sister), and our first joint effort was a song called "The Real American Folk Song Is a Rag," which Nora Bayes sang for a while in *Ladies First*. As this piece was more of an essay than a song it didn't get very far. Finally George got a chance to do a show where he was to be sole composer. It was called *Half-Past Eight* and advertised a Broadway beauty chorus which was nonexistent. With just a few second-hand curtains and sets for production, it opened in Syracuse and was so bad that one critic headed his next morning's review with "Half-Past Eight Not Worth Price of War Tax."

A young producer, Alex Aarons, had great faith in George and in 1919 had him do the complete score for *La, La, Lucille*. This was a smartly conceived musical comedy and the result was quite successful. I recall Victor Jacobi, the light-opera composer, telling George, in the Harms elevator, how much he liked its musical subtleties. Jerome Kern also predicted a great future. That same year, 1919, Caesar and George wrote "Swanee," which, when subsequently introduced by Al Jolson in *Sinbad*, was widely played and purchased.

Beginning in 1920 George wrote, among other things, the music for *George White's Scandals* for five consecutive years. It was for the fourth of this series that he and B. G. DeSylva turned out in six days a short one-act opera called *135th Street*. Lasting only one night, it was eliminated not because it was ineffective artistically but because it changed the mood of the audience, and the tragic note it injected in the proceedings handicapped the gayer numbers that followed. Intimations of the musical paths George was later to follow, especially in recitative, may be found in *135th Street*. It was also in 1923 that Eva Gauthier, with George at the piano, introduced a group of popular and musical-comedy songs at an Aeolian Hall recital. It included numbers by George, Kern, Berlin, and Donaldson. Needless to say, this concert caused quite a commotion in musical circles.

Early in 1924, Paul Whiteman announced a concert with new works by Deems Taylor, Victor Herbert, and George Gershwin. The newspaper item was the first inkling George had that Whiteman was serious when he had once casually mentioned that someday he expected to do such a concert and hoped for a contribution from George. Finding in his notebooks a theme (the clarinet glissando) which he thought might make an appropriate opening for a more extended work than he had been accustomed to writing, he decided to chance it. Three weeks later, with an orchestration by Ferde Grofé, Whiteman was rehearsing *Rhapsody in Blue* in the night club Palais Royal. A week later, when it was presented at Aeolian Hall with the composer at the piano, the response was immediate. Soon it was being played all over the world.

A year after the *Rhapsody* appeared Walter Damrosch commissioned George to compose a work of symphonic scope for the New York Symphony Society. The *Concerto in F* resulted. Incidentally, this was the first time my brother did his own orchestration; all he had ever done in this line was a number or two in *Primrose,* an operetta he wrote in London. To do the scoring of the *Concerto* George rented a couple of rooms at a hotel in order to have comparative quiet from the noisy and busy private house we lived in with the rest of the family. In those two small hotel rooms, within a period of less than three months, he not only orchestrated this work but worked with me on *Tip-Toes* and at the same time collaborated with Herbert Stothart on *Song of the Flame.* All three works had their premières within a few days of each other and, in addition, Whiteman revived *135th Street* in a concert at Carnegie Hall. With George playing six performances of the *Concerto* during that period under Damrosch in New York, Philadelphia, and Baltimore, his energy was seemingly inexhaustible. As he had a very special affection for the *Concerto* it is interesting to note, even if one doesn't believe in artistic yardsticks, that in 1930, when Albert Coates, the eminent English conductor, compiled a list of *Fifty Best Works in Music*, there was included only one American work and that was the *Concerto in F*.

For the firm of Aarons and Freedley, beginning in 1924, George and I did the words and music for seven musical comedies, *Lady, Be Good, Tip-Toes, Oh, Kay!, Funny Face, Treasure Girl, Girl Crazy,* and *Pardon My English;* of these, five were hits and two were failures. In 1926, Edgar Selwyn, having signed George and myself, asked George S. Kaufman if he had an idea for a novel musical. Kaufman said he had a notion for a satire on war, but it probably wouldn't be terribly successful. Selwyn decided to take the chance, and *Strike Up the Band* resulted. Out of town it was hailed by the few but the many stayed away. Rewritten by Morrie Ryskind in 1930, it was the first of the three satirical operettas done by the quartet of Kaufman, Ryskind, and ourselves. The second, produced by Sam H. Harris, was *Of Thee I Sing*, which was awarded the Pulitzer prize in 1932 and was followed by *Let 'Em Eat Cake* in 1933.

In the spring of 1928, George took his fifth and last trip to Europe. With *Funny Face* and *Rosalie* running in New York and *Oh, Kay!* in London, a vacation was in order, and my sister, my wife, and myself accompanied him. I did little other than see sights and drink beer, but George, despite all his social activities, his meetings with many of Europe's important composers, the hours spent with various interviewers and musical critics, still found time to work on *American in Paris* in the hotels we stayed at. The entire "blues" section was written at the Hotel Majestic in Paris. Damrosch sponsored its first performance and it has been popular with symphony organizations ever since.

At the Lewisohn Stadium Concerts in New York George often appeared as soloist, composer, and conductor. One program devoted entirely to his own works, August 16, 1932, attracted an audience of more than 18,000 and set a record for this stadium. At this concert he introduced *Rhumba* (later called *Cuban Overture*) which Pitts Sanborn found superior to Ravel's *Bolero* in musical body. At Ravinia Park and other stadia and concert halls his appearance usually broke local records for attendance. In 1934, he toured with an orchestra conducted by Charles Previn and gave thirty concerts in as many days. In the year 1936 he had more performances of his works played by symphonic organizations than did any other American composer. The greatest gathering ever to crowd the Lewisohn Stadium attended the Memorial Concert in August 1937.

Porgy and Bess, his most ambitious work, was composed in eleven months, and he did the orchestration in nine; during this period he did a good deal of broadcasting. Although most of the opera was done in New York, parts were written in Charleston's Folly Beach, in Westchester, in Palm Beach, on Fire Island, and in the Adirondacks. Sponsored by the Theatre Guild, directed by Rouben Mamoulian, and conducted by Alexander Smallens, it opened in Boston to great acclaim, then played sixteen weeks in New York and followed with a three months' road tour. In 1938, Merle Armitage revived it in Los Angeles and San Francisco with most of the original cast.

Besides his music, George was also interested in painting. He became an ardent collector, specializing in the French moderns and in African sculpture. About 1928 he himself began to paint, and was considered exceedingly capable by professional critics.

Hollywood called again in the summer of 1936 (we had been there in 1930 for the picture *Delicious*) and the Astaire-Rogers film *Shall We Dance?* resulted. This was followed by *A Damsel in Distress*, during which period George learned that he, along with Villa-Lobos, had been elected an honorary member of the Academy of Santa Cecilia, Italy's highest award to foreign composers. Following *Damsel* we were working on *The Goldwyn Follies* when George began to get the headaches which three weeks later proved to be caused by a tumor on his brain. Two days before the operation we were still discussing songs. He died Sunday morning, July 11, 1937, in Los Angeles at the age of thirty-eight.

> *Except for one slight change, the above was written as an article for my 1938 George Gershwin book. Simply and objectively written as it is, it remains, in my opinion, one of the best sketches written about George Gershwin.*
>
> M.A.

★ ★ GEORGE GERSHWIN ★ ★

MAN AND LEGEND

1. The Nature of George Gershwin

I WAS reading in the lounge car of the Super Chief en route back to Los Angeles. During several months in Europe I had acquired information that was very disquieting, especially in Germany, where my every move had been shadowed and where I saw preparations that made war seem inevitable. It was early in July 1937 and it was surprising how little the American press carried about the tense European situation. Suddenly my eye lighted on a heading and paragraph which announced that George Gershwin had been taken to a hospital for an operation.

This simple statement filled me with apprehension. George was such an active, athletic, healthy young man. What on earth had sent him to a hospital? Nevertheless, I could not cast off the foreboding.

Immediately upon my arrival I telephoned the Gershwin home and was referred to the hospital. Calling the hospital, I asked for Ira and was informed he had just left. Then I heard the operator say, "This is Merle Armitage on the telephone. Shall I tell him?" With fear in my heart I waited interminable seconds. Then a voice said, "George Gershwin passed away five minutes ago."

George Gershwin dead!

In the taxi going to my office it was extremely difficult for me to accept and assimilate this shocking fact. Following the first stab of pain at losing such an admired friend came the question of his great projected composition for the string quartet. What had happened to that? It would be a bitter irony if George's schedule had not enabled him to carry out his plan to get it down on paper. Not wanting to introduce this subject to Ira at the moment, when I arrived at my office I called Harold Arlen, one of George's close friends, to find out if he knew about the quartet. Arlen answered the phone himself: not one single note had been written.

George had worked on the quartet, entirely in his mind, for many, many months. He could play any passage in it at will, and he played many of them for me, but he had not committed a note to paper. While he had been working at R.K.O. on his last picture, and busy with many other projects, the string quartet had begun to evolve. He had kept it in a separate compartment in his mind, and everywhere and at any time that even a five-minute opportunity occurred he was busy building another phrase of it or adding another element to one of its movements.

George Gershwin had reached unusual musical maturity. His most important work, *Porgy and Bess,* was behind him. What a rich and amazing contribution he might have made to the literature of string quartets!

The next few months, if sorrowful, were hectic. In 1937 I had promised George and Ira that I would produce *Porgy and Bess* on the West Coast. The preliminary arrangements, large and small, were absorbing. And I had resolved to undertake another Gershwin project, a book about the man and his work. Now that George was gone, his great accomplishments packed into a surprisingly small number of years, a restatement and a summing up seemed necessary. As the plan for the book took shape, all of Gershwin's friends and associates were called upon for articles, and the book developed into a major project. All, without exception, wanted to testify to their friendship for George and their admiration for his music. But most of them had never written a line, and here they were being asked to make statements in print for posterity. Nonetheless the book, *George Gershwin*, was finally completed, with more than thirty-five distinguished persons contributing. It was published in 1938, enjoyed a substantial public interest, and is now a collectors' item.

Immersed as I was in all these Gershwin activities, in addition to my own impresario and publishing ventures, my mind kept going back over the Gershwin career. It was such a singular career, and so short. And George was such a distinguished, talented, and unusual human being. I had never known anyone remotely resembling him. Thankful as I was for having known and worked with him, I seemed always to return to the accident of our meeting.

It was at some time in the 1920's. I had become conscious of a distinguished-looking young man whom I encountered frequently during my visits to the art galleries. This young man always smoked a pipe and usually was with an attractive woman. Their comments about pictures were discerning. They were a fascinating pair.

This couple came into the Weyhe Gallery on Lexington Avenue one morning and I asked Carl Zigrosser, the director, who they were. He promptly introduced me to George Gershwin and Miss Kay Swift. We had a few moments of amusing conversation recalling our many encounters in galleries. After I had offered compliments to George on his delightful music, which he accepted with genuine embarrassment, we went our separate ways.

Those, too, were busy days for me. Not only was I managing the concert appearances of John McCormack and Galli-Curci all over the United States, but in many large American cities I had established concert courses that presented artists under my management plus attractions managed by other New York agencies. It was during this period that Antonia Scotti, the best friend of Gatti-Casazza, the impresario of the Metropolitan Opera, persuaded that astute gentleman to allow Scotti and myself to form a touring opera company. We engaged many of the top Metropolitan stars, such as Geraldine Farrar, Martinelli, Chamlee, De Luca, Florence Easton, and others, and "borrowed" the Met's scenery, costumes, and minor artists. Three tours of the United States in 1919, 1920, and 1921 were made as the Scotti Grand Opera Company. Later we persuaded Mary Garden to return from Europe before the beginning of her fall season with the Chicago Opera and do concert tours. That was a very exciting business.

The period of the twenties was the golden age of musical concerts in the United States. Theatrical companies were giving up tours because of burgeoning motion-picture competition, there was no television, and radio was in its infancy: hams with crystal sets in Denver were getting sounds from Pittsburgh, and vice versa. The phonograph record had put victrolas in every home. Opera singers were recording popular music and thereby building a greater public. Concert singers on tour gave the public one opportunity of hearing and seeing the great musicians. The result: large and eager audiences that overflowed the largest auditoriums.

I came into this exotic business by accident and it rapidly became my profession. In 1911 my family was living in Detroit. I had given up civil engineering because of bad eyesight and the theater had attracted me. It was the time of Belasco, and stage *décor* maintained absolute fidelity to nature and reality: every limb on every tree, every twig on every limb, every leaf on every twig, and every bug on every leaf. That was theater? Not for me.

I began a campaign for the use of imagination in the theater (not knowing that Appia and Gordon Craig existed), and my sketches used a minimum of scenery and props. A flying buttress with curtains and drapes was sufficient for *Tristan and Isolde.* Let the singers and actors have a chance to be seen. That was my dictum. The sketches, immature but practical, were very advanced for that day.

Charles L. Wagner, the manager of Alice Nielsen, David Bispham, Eugen Ysaye, and other concert celebrities of the time, came to town. A friend of mine insisted on showing him my work because Wagner was also a producer of plays, having Jeffery Farnol's *The Money Moon* on the road at the time. Wagner was impressed. He insisted on showing them to Ben Hampton of *Cosmopolitan* magazine and Hampton bought them to illustrate an article on new trends in the theater. Selling drawings to national magazines at eighteen years of age was heady experience, but it was just the beginning.

Three weeks later a telegram came from Charles L. Wagner asking if I were available to manage a festival in Appleton, Wisconsin. My telegraphed reply said, "I'm on my way to Appleton, but what is a festival?"

Momentarily baffled when I discovered that I must raise ten thousand dollars by lining up a group of guarantors, I tackled the local banker. First he signed my subscription list, and the rest was reasonably easy.

I then studied the festival program and its problems. The festival was to consist of a week of music by the Minneapolis Symphony Orchestra, with such soloists as Leopold Godowsky, the pianist (father of Leopold Godowsky, Jr., coinventor of Kodachrome, who married George Gershwin's sister), Nellie Melba, and Clarence Whitehill, bass. Melba, of course, was the magnet who sold tickets. Everything went well. All my errors, all the *faux pas* of an amateur, were hidden in the general and unexpected success. At Appleton I had my first lesson in writing publicity releases, counting the box office, and the care and feeding of prima donnas.

With the Appleton festival yielding a profit to its sponsor, the Lawrence Conservatory of Music, Wagner promptly assigned me to other and more difficult situations. After three years of this, we became partners. The sensational John McCormack, Emmy Destinn, Frances Alda, Galli-Curci, and later Gieseking, came under our management. The late Will Rogers, whom we took from the *Ziegfeld Follies* for a "lecture" tour, added another hilarious chapter to our tumultuous days.

Gershwin's success was woven through the coruscating fabric of my life in these years. Morris Gest had invited me to the opening of his *Midnight Whirl* at the Century Theatre in December 1919, and Gershwin's contribution to the show made an impression. I instructed my office to watch the papers while I was on the road and to notify me of any Gershwin work or performance of any kind.

One evening in August of 1922 my train to New York was late and as a result my arrival at the Globe Theatre for the opening of the *Scandals of 1922* coincided with the rise of the curtain; I had not even had time for dinner. Included in this *Scandals* potpourri was Gershwin's *Blue Monday*, now known as his one-act opera *135th Street*. The audience had never heard anything like it. The next two or three numbers, comparative froth, made little impression on me. On the way out of the theater I purchased three tickets for the following night, so that friends might enjoy with me the new mood of *Blue Monday*: jazz in somewhat operatic form.

We waited in vain throughout that second performance. No *Blue Monday*. The producers had seen the devastating effect of this compelling work upon the rest of their show and had withdrawn it. The other acts could not stand up to the impact of *Blue Monday*.

My appetite for Gershwin grew. Two years later the office wired me about a forthcoming Gershwin appearance. He and Paul Whiteman would collaborate in Aeolian Hall. In Los Angeles, where I was organizing the Los Angeles Grand Opera Association, I managed to get the last available space on the Chief. This put me into New York the morning of this debut. I spent the day with Catherine Bamman, manager of Carlos Salzedo, Georges Barrère, Povla Frijsh, and other aristocratic artists, and we went to the first performance of the *Rhapsody in Blue*. Bamman was strictly a classicist. She thought the performance was indeed a lot of fun but that it belonged in a night club. We discussed this at dinner and until two o'clock in the morning, for I had heard a new and triumphal signal, long awaited.

"This work has a great future," I argued, "and George Gershwin has a great destiny."

"Perhaps you are right, Merle, but please eliminate the word *great*."

We closed on that note. I was certain that a new and very American voice had emerged.

By some alchemy I attended many of the Gershwin performances which made history, including *Our Nell*, which contained the song "*Innocent Ingenue Baby*," in 1922; *Lady, Be Good*, with lyrics by Ira Gershwin in 1924. If I missed *Song*

Paul Whiteman, by Auerbach-Levy

of the Flame and *Tell Me More,* I caught *Tip-Toes, Oh, Kay!*
In 1925, when Walter Damrosch and his orchestra presented
Concerto in F, it was impossible for me to attend, but the concerto has become one of my favorite works, so characteristic
is it of George's style. When Damrosch conducted *An American in Paris* at Carnegie Hall in December 1928, I heard the

first performance of this work which has enjoyed such popularity, but charming as it is, it never seemed to me the most important of Gershwin's works.

Even though I missed a few productions with Gershwin music, fortunately I witnessed some of the greatest shows ever to invade Broadway. They must be favorites of thousands who were in New York in the early 1930's. Unforgettable were *Strike Up the Band, Girl Crazy, Of Thee I Sing,* and *Let 'Em Eat Cake.* These performances had a verve, a spontaneity, and an overpowering enthusiasm seldom achieved in the theater. Those who saw them will remember; those who did not, have missed theater never to be exactly duplicated.

There were two song recitalists who intrigued me in this period, Povla Frijsh and Eva Gauthier. Watching the schedules of their appearances, I endeavored to be on hand for them. Both singers were unique as artists, and Eva Gauthier had a special fascination for me, because of her explorations into contemporary song writing. At one of her recitals I heard for the first time songs by a group of such advanced composers as Schoenberg, Milhaud, Hindemith, and Bartók.

Some time in 1923 Eva Gauthier gave a program (I have worn out the printed copy) devoted to jazz. Only a singer with her prestige and following could have ventured such an audacious business. I attended this most important event with an old friend, a pianist, whom I had first heard in Boston and then booked on national tours, the inimitable George Copeland. George and I had a wonderful afternoon although our pleasure was not shared by some in the audience. There were songs by Jerome Kern and by Irving Berlin, sounding very fine indeed in Aeolian Hall. There were at least three Gershwin songs and Eva Gauthier gave them a very special treatment, with George himself as her accompanist. They were all tumultuously received. The encore remains freshest in my mind, the delicious "Do It Again." During dinner with George Copeland that evening there was scarcely a word of conversation not relating to the exciting events of the afternoon.

Scanning the papers the next day for the critics' reaction, I was delighted to read Deems Taylor in the New York World. He did not hesitate to commit himself: "It seemed to one listener that the jazz numbers stood up amazingly well, not only as entertainment but as music. . . . What they did possess was melodic interest and continuity-harmonic appropriateness, well-balanced, almost classically severe form, and subtle and fascinating rhythm—in short, the qualities that any sincere and interesting music possesses." And Carl Van Vechten, one of the most fastidious listeners, wrote: "I consider this one of the very most important events in American musical history."

Around the same time Beryl Rubinstein, a major pianist and a composer, gave an interview that was widely published because of its daring and conviction: "With Gershwin's style and seriousness he is not definitely of the popular-music school, but is one of the really outstanding figures in this country's serious musical efforts. . . . This young man has great charm and a most magnetic personality, and I really believe that America will at no distant date honor him for his talent . . . and that when we speak of American composers George Gershwin's name will be prominent on our list."

I was myself a confirmed Gershwin addict by then with a strong conviction that George Gershwin was a greater prophet of a new music than any other American. Even if Broadway was his by right of eminent domain, he had already emerged from the aspic of musical shows. Although he was the most facile and tender and captivating song writer of his time, nevertheless his larger works for the concert halls were tantalizing and they held a powerful promise of greater things to come. The greatest of these did come in the autumn of 1935, when *Porgy and Bess* opened in Boston and then proceeded to New York.

George Gershwin arrived on the scene during one of the most turbulent and amazing periods in American history. Everything was being changed or questioned. Alert scientists, engineers, and other professionals knew, or suspected, the revolution that was about to happen, as did some writers, painters, and composers. But certainly the general public was unaware of it.

George came in time to put his shoulder to the wheel and make his singular contribution. He "belonged" to the fresh, young, eager F. Scott Fitzgerald generation, seeking every sort of emancipation from the comparative stuffy environment of the period.

Just how stuffy, pretentious, and dull had been the lives of most people in the period before this revolution got under way, it is now hard to believe. American millionaires enjoyed the rococo splendor of Newport homes. Upper Fifth Avenue, the north Lake Shore of Chicago, and Nob Hill in San Francisco were areas of ostentatious wealth. Mansions were filled with bogus or imitation art: furniture, bric-à-brac, sculpture, murals, glass panels, and whatnot. It was all European or imitation of European modes. Luxurious private cars were numbered in the hundreds, and America had a kind of gaudy brashness that was amusing if somewhat oppressive.

As for the rest of the population, most Americans were under the spell of this cast-iron crudity. Our country was in a state of emerging from a rustic or rural into a more urban culture, and, as was natural, most of the people so caught were decidedly ill at ease. In the seventies, concentrated money and its pretentiousness which had characterized that period were wearing off. The middle class inherited this flimsy façade and went in for gaudiness on a large scale. Suburb and "bungalow" development spread over most of America with appalling results. Furniture "genuinely veneered" appeared, as did a packing-case style known as Mission. Shades of Elbert Hubbard! On tables and other surfaces, objects of plaster, gilt, wicker, bamboo, burnt leather and wood, punched brass, hand-painted china took their place as "Arts and Crafts" dominated our decorations. Old tennis rackets, gilded, hung on walls, and little blown-glass ships, horses, under glass hoods, were chic things on "parlor" tables. There were potted palms in jardinières and tabourets were popular in "dens." Gas mantels shed a green radiance over rooms hung with paintings of lions, framed with wooden bars in imitation of cages. Wallpaper of hideous, garish design made every room *busy* to the point of distraction. Every bad accessory was an imitation of some bad, if genuine, example.

Being born into this milieu gives me very sharp and accurate pictures of the period. Well I remember American residential streets, trees meeting overhead to form an arch, resounding with little piano pieces, Chaminade, McDowell, and the rest, played by reluctant pupils on out-of-tune pianos. All the absurdities that a newly industrialized Europe had experienced at a slightly earlier period were repeated in dreary facsimile and with added horrors here in America.

Everything was affected. Literature had been characterized by a "seedy conservatism." Aesthetic appreciation, strictly on European lines and of a rather exhibitionistic nature, was rampant and was epitomized by Huneker. Mencken was just

Caricature of G. G. at the piano, by M. A.

Components of jazz, by M. A.

about to attack the smoldering ignorance and intolerance of the Bible Belt, and yellow journalism held its sway. The one beacon of light and interest that signaled the emergence of a new America was *The Dial*. e. e. cummings in one of his Harvard nonlectures says: "Through Harvard, I met Scotfield Thayer, and at Harvard, Sibley Watson—two men who subsequently transformed a do-gooding periodical called *The Dial* into a first-rate magazine of the fine arts; and together fought the eternal fight of selfhood against mobism, the immortal battle of beauty against ugliness."

This was the soil that had been prepared for the advent of Gershwin. Here it should be said that even the cynics, the unbelievers, and the critics of progress in America must, if honest, admit that in less than sixty years a miracle has been wrought. I do not speak of material progress, but of the growth and development of other values. All the things that were so hateful to sensitive men have been repudiated by the most amazing and thorough transformation of cultural standards in history.

Our young students in public schools today are subjected to Cézanne, Picasso, Braque, and the best American painters; they hear the music of Stravinsky, Schoenberg, Bartók, and Gershwin; the school itself is a modern, simple, and beautiful structure with adequate light and air. There is more real culture per capita in America today than there has ever been anywhere else at any time.

What brought about this unprecedented change? The hopeless morass, with its ignorance, tawdry furnishings, unsightly buildings, and sprawling growth, was attacked by a group of remarkable men and women, courageous and ingenious. Today they assume monumental stature. Nor did they band together; many of them never heard of the other champions. They went ahead alone and in their own fields. They unconsciously formed what General Doolittle describes as "a company front."

Frank Lloyd Wright attacked with genius, logic, new materials, and a fierce conviction the whole concept of architecture, or the lack of it, in the United States. Other men, Lescaze, Howe, Neutra, Saarinen, and the younger men who followed, helped to change the profile of America. With their changes in architecture, changes in ideas, vision, and scope were bound to follow.

Edward Weston fought the battle in the realm of photography. He met and conquered the stupidly held opinion that it was the medium used, not the *result*, that made art. Edward Weston photographs, which have opened new vistas of aesthetics, are now the treasured possessions of our greatest museums and in the portfolios of discerning collectors. His influence was immense.

John Marin, independent American painter, fighting the ridicule of unseeing eyes, made his revolution in extracting the spirit of this country and giving it verisimilitude and beautiful coherence. *S. Macdonald Wright* made a similar contribution, beginning with his development of "Synchromie" in Paris about 1912, and continuing through to his present powerful abstractions.

Martha Graham created a new school of the dance through employment of natural laws and made crystal clear the meaning of movement in space. Her pupils and followers have vitally changed the spirit of the dance.

And *George Gershwin* proved conclusively that on this continent can emerge a music expressing a new spirit. He belongs with the brave group who were the first to light the fires. I am not underestimating the vast and vital contributions of European-born men and women who contributed their genius to this country. There are Europeans who were born into a spirit so akin to that germinating in America as to be blood relations. They were drawn to America as a magnet attracts steel. Stravinsky, Schoenberg, Varèse, Bartók, have exerted powerful influence on their adopted land.

The seed of these things was planted deep. It was a long time finding its proper and natural soil. It goes back to the beginning, when freedom and bare survival occupied men's minds, energies, and hearts to the exclusion of all else. But if dormant and sleeping, it was nevertheless there.

The differences in the European and American thinking and concepts of life are subtle and often difficult to explain, but an article written by Otto H. Kahn offers a striking illustration of the basic conflict and contrast. First let me explain the author, who was a great admirer of Gershwin. Otto H. Kahn was a brilliant financier, head of Kuhn, Loeb and Company, chairman of the Board of the Metropolitan Opera Company, and the most diligent and generous patron of the arts and show business. Kahn was the great angel, the man who was always ready to help a cause if he thought it worthy. Through my dealings with the Metropolitan Opera he and I often came into contact. Seldom does one meet a more intelligent and ready response, or a more gallant reception, than Kahn had to offer. But Otto H. Kahn had another side. He could be, and often was, the author of a very golden yield of bathos. This was a sort of hangover from the nineties, a time when affectation was often confused with affection, when sentimentality posed as sentiment.

One of the European ideas that gained a firm hold in this

country was that America could never be great until it had
"suffered." Let me therefore quote Kahn on this subject, se-
lecting several extracts from *Appreciation,* which he wrote
of George Gershwin in 1929, a remarkable document:

The path of America—since she became a nation—has been
all too smooth perhaps, too uniformly successful. Mercifully, she
has been spared in her development the ordeal of deep anguish,
besetting care, and heart-searching tribulations which mark the
history of older nations—except only the epic tragedy of Civil
War.

... Now, far be it from me to wish any tragedy to come into
the life of this nation for the sake of chastening its soul, or into
the life of George Gershwin for the sake of deepening his art.
But I do want to quote to him a few verses (by Thomas Hardy,
I believe) which I came across the other day and which are
supposed to relate to America:

> I shrink to see a modern coast
> Whose riper times have yet to be;
> Where the new regions claim them free
> From that long drip of human tears
> Which people old in tragedy
> Have left upon the centuried years.

The *long drip of human tears,* my dear George! They have great
and strange and beautiful power, those human tears. They
fertilize the deepest roots of art, and from them flowers spring
of a loveliness and perfume that no other moisture can produce.

... I could wish for you an experience—not too prolonged—
of that driving storm and stress of the emotions, of that solitary
wrestling with your own soul, of that aloofness, for a while,
from the actions and distractions of the everyday world, which
are the most effective ingredients for the deepening and mellow-

ing and the complete development, energizing, and revealment of an artist's inner being and spiritual powers.

Does this bathos, masked as philosophy, really apply to the world generally, and to George Gershwin in particular? Essentially, it must be false doctrine. The suffering of Europe has brought a disorganization of almost all functions, a bitterness, a frustration that is bringing it to the brink of ruin. And is the percentage of great artists thereby raised?

No amount of suffering, obviously, is going to deepen or mellow or in any way help a human being who is not gifted or equipped with a deep sensibility. Great sorrow or strain can destroy these qualities. We are the inheritors of a tradition that what is worth while must be dull, says Gilbert Seldes, and as often as not we invert the maxim and pretend that what is dull is higher in quality, more serious, "greater art," in short, than whatever is light and gay.

Had Otto H. Kahn really looked at George Gershwin, or understood his music, he would have been surprised. Deep in the being of George Gershwin was a map of all the human suffering of the world. Anyone who knew him could not have missed that characteristic feature. The music of Gershwin is essentially a refutation of all that is base, mean, ugly, defeated, and supine. George declared for a better world, a joyous brotherhood, a synthesis of what is best in the human concept. This is a component of everything he wrote. Possibly some of it is naïve, innocent, and playful. But his meaning is clear.

Who but a man who subconsciously is laden with sorrow and with beneficient love could have written the music which is *Porgy and Bess?* Either a man has the qualities necessary for an artist or he does not. As Spinoza, who would have understood George Gershwin, says: "The courage to be is not one thing besides others. It is an expression of the essential act of everything that participates in being, namely *self-affirmation*. Virtue is the power of acting exclusively according to one's *true nature*."

The George Gershwin confidence, which was far from egotism as commonly understood, is a characteristic of many great artists. Da Vinci possessed it, as did Michelangelo. Picasso has it vividly. Stravinsky stated this Olympian concept very simply when, in 1934, he wrote: "I am on a perfectly sure road; there is nothing to discuss or criticize. One does not criticize anyone that is functioning."

2. Discoveries
and Inventions

IT IS difficult, if not impossible, to find a category for Gershwin. Reading an obscure speech by Abraham Lincoln, I came across a statement that seemed to express what I feel about composers. He said: "Man is not the only animal who labors; but he is the only animal who *improves* his work. This improvement he effects by DISCOVERIES AND INVENTIONS."

There we have it. We have composers who discover, and we have composers who invent. George Gershwin is *both* a discoverer and an inventor. He is a *discoverer* in the sense that he has infused his music with that vitality, directness of approach, democratic understanding, and comparative informality which are among the American contributions to our time. His greatest *invention* is the introduction of a new style based on the meaning of man, the emotional response of human beings.

George was not a prodigy, but he certainly was a phenomenon. Actually he was supercharged with music. It was not immodesty, as many people supposed, but an inner and irresistible compulsion that drove him night and day. On the tennis courts, on the golf course, swimming, or driving a car, George Gershwin was a musical volcano that insisted on erupting. Take the night he went to Boston for the première of one of his works; in the natural rhythm of the locomotive exhaust, the muffled clickety-click-click of the wheels of the Pullman, punctuated with the whistle for crossings—provided the springboard for a new composition. Most of the things he experienced in life were somehow related to his inevitable purposes.

If, as psychologists have proven, the average healthy and active mind is subconsciously preoccupied with problems, ideas, plans, organizations, comparisons, evaluations, and the review of past events and forecasts of things to come, then the less cerebral but more creative mind of the composer generates sounds, combinations of sounds, and new arrangements of sounds which clamor for release and attention night and day. These *sounds* in the case of a Gershwin emerge as music.

To make clear what we mean by "Discovery versus Invention," let us look at Sibelius and Rachmaninoff, for example. Each has written beautiful, ingratiating, stirring, and noble music—has enriched musical literature. But it in no way negates their work to understand it as but remotely connected with contemporary music. Their compositions are within the boundaries of the known musical world. Rachmaninoff has remained within the musical area defined by Chopin, Borodin, and Schumann. Sibelius did not surpass the confines explored by Berlioz, Brahms, and Debussy.

Each is a member of the Romantic school, grouped with the *discovery* rather than with the *invention* composers. Both have *discovered* wonderful new ways of stating emotional truth in well-defined forms. They are not singled out as apart—the interesting works of the Soviet composer Dimitri Shostakovich, for example, do not venture beyond previously explored musical latitudes—they are simply selected as particularly splendid examples of a school of great composers who represent one attitude and approach.

But Varèse, Bartók, Stravinsky, Schoenberg, and Gershwin have invented new forms, although each did it in a very different way.

Even though Varèse is not an American composer, he is certainly composing in America. Years ago in his thick-walled Burgundy home he could hear in imagination the whistles of locomotives far out on the American prairie and knew he was destined for this country. His music is immense, powerful, and significant; it parallels the great forces of nature, the enormous movements of the cosmos, a world of organized anarchy. It is perhaps the most universal music yet enunciated, universal in the sense of the grandeur of the universe, absolute music.

Bartók compositions are vigorous and fresh in sounds. Through an enormous knowledge of his country's folk music he has been able to convey a peasantlike sense of reality, combining a bitter feeling of violence with a gentle playfulness, in his own *inventive* way of writing music.

Stravinsky's inventions are based on a pungent world, the soil, the erotic stirrings of spring, the imaginative-physical world, the primitiveness and mystery lying just beneath the surface of civilized man.

Schoenberg's music is austere. Its scholarly background, its mathematical, constellation-like form, its startling abridgments, its penetration, regardless of the pitfalls for habit-trained ears, achieve a peak of exultation and conjuration not encountered in the work of any living composer organized in the same direction.

Gershwin's invention lies in variation of rhythm, new placement of accent, new emphasis and color. In his songs, to the heretofore metallic, strident jazz he brought a quality of delicacy, even dreaminess.

Discoverers throughout history have made a contribution
as valuable as that of the *inventors*. History gives each his
proper place and honor. In their own time and generation,
discoverers fare much better than do the inventors, irrespective
of their various fields of activity. Rachmaninoff and Sibelius
have been widely acclaimed—their music is much more literary, much easier for our habit-trained ears to comprehend. We
have been conditioned to them by the men who preceded
them. But for the works of the inventors there is little precedent.

When Toscanini elected to play the music of living composers, it was the works of Respighi, Casella, or Ravel, the more
literary, lyric music writers, rather than of the men who have
pushed back musical horizons. And when he did play the
Rhapsody in Blue over the NBC network in November 1942
it was generally agreed that he missed the meaning and significance of the work. Virgil Thomson said: "It all came off like
a ton of bricks." However, to do him credit, Toscanini confided
more than once to Samuel Chotzinoff that "Gershwin is the
only *real* American music."

But it must be said that many conductors have had the
courage to champion new composers. Koussevitzky, Rodzinski,
Goossens, Beecham, Krueger, Klemperer, Damrosch, and particularly Stokowski and Bernstein are but a few of the maestros
who have been sympathetic to the changing world.

The modern inventor-composers, diverse in form, attitude,
and results, share one consistency: compactness of structure.

Certain pages in Stravinsky's *Le Sacre du Printemps*, in
Schoenberg's *Verklaerte Nacht*, in Bartók's *Quartet N° 1 in
A Minor*, in Hindemith's *Der Schwanendreher*, in Satie's
Gymnopédie, in Varèse's *Amériques*, in Gershwin's *Concerto*

Three Themes [Autograph] from the Operatized *Blue Monday Blues*

in F, and even certain sections in the score of Prokofieff's *The Love for Three Oranges*, introduce and then abandon enough thematic material to enable some present-day follower of Schubert to fashion several full-length symphonies.

Repetition is also renounced. The device of the classic composers is absent in contemporary music, as is the cornice in modern architecture. The strategy of introducing a theme, repeating it thereafter with variations through the choirs and instruments of the orchestra, has enabled composers from before the day of Mozart to after that of Wagner to erect a magnificent number of musical edifices against the ostensibly scant number of contributions by contemporary men. The brilliant exception (in prolificness of compact musical ideas or themes) is the early inventor, Johann Sebastian Bach.

The condensation achieved by the moderns must be taken into account in measuring the comparative opera of men who have written important music. It must be remembered, also, that early composers had the entire field before them, have therefore appropriated a tremendous proportion of the possible musical material, as music is now constituted. The man who makes a new and original musical statement today is indeed remarkable.

The fact that George Gershwin was a Jew and that many of his musical sources were Negroid confirms his basic Americanism. For this is not a country of race, it is a country of amalgamated races.

The natural excitement, nervousness, and movement of America were indigenous motivations in Gershwin's life and Gershwin's music. It is a commonplace that during his lifetime his music had little discerning critical appraisal. Admirers and friends, the thousands who had fallen in love with his music, the very *enthusiasm* which Gershwin engendered, crowded out the possibility and opportunity for detached, considered evaluation. George confused everybody, because he was unique.

America had almost overcome its musical inferiority complex, through its possession of more first-class symphony orchestras than could be heard in *all* of Europe, when its smugness suffered a little shock. A denizen of Tin Pan Alley was first tolerated, then *invited* into the temples of great music.

Although many European critics had long since recognized the vitality of American jazz, and had written of the extreme probability that jazz and the technique of jazz would affect the constitution of the symphony orchestra and composition of the future, we were much too complacent with our foreign importations to risk admiring a home-grown product, and much too unsure of its importance. We were also unaware that jazz had exerted a great influence on European art. Indeed, Negroism, from Gauguin to Modigliani, to Picasso and Derain, has had many followers in painting. Debussy wrote more than one "cakewalk" even before 1914. The influence is apparent in certain early works of Stravinsky, Milhaud, and Hindemith. Intellectual Europe had recognized the first convincing aesthetic American development.

The situation in the United States was quite different. Because jazz had been quickly accepted by people generally as a natural expression, the more informed public, as well as the critics, had tabulated and abandoned it as a rhythmical expression for bestial instincts in all their primitive force, and nothing more. We have forgotten the tumult and the shouting which existed in the early 1920's in regard to the decadence of the jazz age. Reactionaries of both continents found jazz a most satisfactory target for their invective. Case in point: in London, on October 8, 1927, Sir Henry Coward, one of England's leading musicians and a world authority on choral technique, said "a lowering of our moral standards and a consequent loss of the prestige of the white race in the world" would be among the dire results of the vogue for jazz. We had not recognized that anything vital, anything convincing, anything truly important in American art must have its roots in our own soil and our own environment. Lacking insight and awareness, we did not perceive, to quote Louis Danz's neat sentence, that "a season with André Lhote might *not* make an American painter nor a prize scholarship with Nadia Boulanger an American composer."

Into this milieu the figure of George Gershwin was projected. Already in certain quarters he was damned, for he had written the outrageously successful "Swanee" for Al Jolson, and several of *George White's Scandals.*

There were other American composers—living and dead. But they were imitative, not only of the methods of Europe but of its spirit—a spirit which was and is decadent. These composers had attempted to cover their weaknesses of spurious inspiration with inventions, with external showiness which often deceived the unknowing. As a matter of fact, even today the long arm of Europe still stretches its deadening hand of tradition, still exercises its authority over many American developments, causing the true spirit of America to be submerged. To follow the MacDowells, the Parkers, the Cadmans, and the Hadleys of the past and the present, who have taken over a foreign art ready made and are imitating it with some success but with a complete absence of vital force, *is not the future,* therefore, of the American composer. That future will be captured by the contemporary-minded American whose awareness has apprised him of our divergence; the man who knows that ours is a different but not an inferior contribution, who has abandoned academic romanticism, and who knows that there is such a thing as the aesthetic of the engineers and architects.

A number of highly endowed individuals among American composers, men who were aware of trends on both sides of the Atlantic, were beginning to have an influence in American music; they were restricted, however, to a comparatively small group. Roger Sessions, George Antheil, Aaron Copland, Louis Gruenberg, Charles Ives, and later Roy Harris, had changed the entire picture of American composition and given it a new prestige. But these men were at an impasse. They were without an audience.

Gershwin came to bat, so to speak, with the bleachers full.

When the New York Symphony Society, through Walter Damrosch, commissioned Gershwin to compose a work of symphonic proportions, it resulted in the *Concerto in F*. When, in turn, this work was heard in Carnegie Hall, with Damrosch conducting and the composer at the piano, the capacity audience was synthetic—consisting of one-third curious intellectuals, one-third conservative subscribers, and one-third Gershwin devotees. Gershwin, from the time Paul Whiteman had programmed the *Rhapsody in Blue*, never was without an audience. The musical purists, however, found George in many respects inadequate. Among the more frequently heard criticisms were that he was unable to sustain a phrase more than sixteen or thirty-two bars long, the clumsiness of his orchestrations, that his arias were ill formed (*Porgy and Bess*), and that there were other faults in the fundamentals of structure. To use a very hackneyed but telling phrase, the critics were unable to see the forest for the trees. George brought to serious consideration a new idiom in music, and forever changed its future direction.

Let us superficially investigate the anatomy of jazz. If ragtime was a homophonic horizontal music, jazz, at its boldest, is polyphonic, polyrhythmic, and vertical. One authority says jazz is a compound of (a) the fox-trot rhythm, a four-four measure (*alla breve*) with a double accent, and (b) a syncopated melody over this rhythm. However, no mere formula will make jazz. As an illustration, a highly syncopated line like the second subject in César Franck's *Symphony in D Minor* or the principal theme of Beethoven's third *Leonore* overture is merely syncopation until you add to it the heavy bump-bump of the fox-trot beat. The combination, on the authority of Virgil Thomson, is jazz. It is a mistake to speak of jazz as a product of the Negro, although its primary associations, such as its rhythm, are black and derive ultimately from the African South. In the course of its filtration from the South to the cosmopolitan world it has undergone a metamorphosis, and in its development it has certainly been touched and influenced by the Hebrew.

There is considerable evidence of the fact that something approaching modern jazz existed six or seven hundred years ago. It was an epoch when men in music began to realize dimly what an amazing effect could be made by a number of people singing different things at the same time. Not being expert in combining different melodic strands, they experimented with a sort of catch-as-catch-can discant. The serious composers attacked the then colossal task of making two or three familiar tunes harmonize, and the result, we hazard, would not have been unfamiliar to modern ears. Nor is orchestral improvisation an invention of our age. Three hundred years ago the musicians in the orchestras of Monteverdi and Peri were expected to improvise counterpoint. They possessed this talent to such a degree that the more or less skeleton scores of these operas which have been saved can give us only an imperfect idea of how this music actually sounded in performance.

An orchestra like that of Paul Whiteman is in a sense a return, in a contemporary manner, to certain ancient conceptions of the orchestra. In the Whiteman band instruments have no privileges; all the artists are equal and all timbres are valued alike. There are no more technical prejudices; a trumpet equals a violincello, a saxophone may eclipse a violin, or a glockenspiel may be on a par with a Stradivarius. It is a magnificent collaboration in which each instrument is merely a

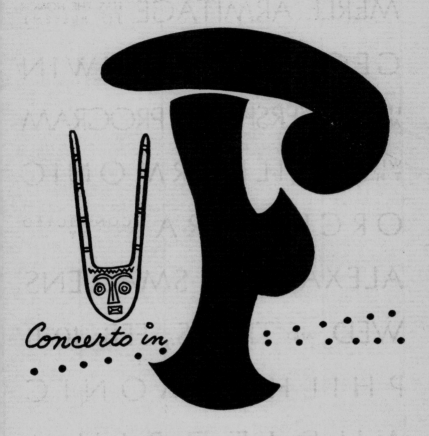

Concerto in ꞏ F

Overtones of the *Concerto in F*, by M. A.

MERLE ARMITAGE HAS THE HONOR TO PRESENT

GEORGE GERSHWIN

IN AN ALL GERSHWIN PROGRAM

WITH THE PHILHARMONIC

ORCHESTRA CONDUCTED BY

ALEXANDER SMALLENS

WED. AND THURS., FEB. 10-11

PHILHARMONIC

AUDITORIUM

Program of the final G. G. concert, designed by M. A.

tube of color at the disposal of the painter, who does not pretend that yellow is superior to blue, or that violet is more respectable than green.

The advent of Gershwin gave rise to a curious attitude on the part of certain people in the musical world. One school of thought held that jazz, after all, might contain something of value, but that only a modern Wagner or Debussy, a *real* composer, could make important use of it. Another school, of course, banned it altogether. But certain influential people of discernment believed that Gershwin *was* a *real* composer—and knew that his music was well founded. There is an attitude today, which has gained some credence, that the "larger" Gershwin works will not live, that only his songs and less pretentious compositions have the seed of immortality.

It seems to me that the question of immortality has been overstressed in every generation. Striving for permanence seems to be an incorrigible human necessity. It is difficult or impossible for us to accept the fact that immortality is relative. Often when confronted by great works of art, or moved by great music, we are inclined to say and believe that such things will never die. Yet immortality is probably only the symbol of some imperishable illusion, for measured in history's vast panorama the fecundity of some new phase certainly means the death of a now discarded one. It is conceivable that in past generations great music was written, and great art created, of which not one fragment remains. Yet that great music and that great art must have been necessary and helpful to the immediate following creators, and in this wise perhaps attained a sort of immortality. George Gershwin opened a musical door through which future composers can enter with comparative ease.

When he proclaimed himself a "modern romantic," Gershwin used the precise term to describe best his attitude and his music. He considered that his discoveries had begun with some nucleus or kernel of material, which for unconscious reasons had taken possession of him.

At the time, Stravinsky had emerged from the earlier "magic orchestra" days of *The Fire Bird* (*L'Oiseau de Feu*), the sonorous masses and unpitying rhythms of *The Rite of Spring* (*Le Sacre du Printemps*), and entered the more neo-classic world of *Octuor, Oedipus,* and *Apollon Musagète*.

Schoenberg had passed *Pierrot Lunaire* and the *Gurrelieder* and was deep in his laboratory of Twelve-Tone Music. Bartók was being introduced to America. Mary Wigman had developed a new dance attitude in Europe, and Martha Graham had forsaken the sentimentalities of the Denishawn school; she had created and performed the astringent *Frontier*.

Painters following the Armory show were abandoning silky landscapes in hot pursuit of Picasso and non-figurative art. Almost without exception, serious American composers were deployed along the Stravinsky-Schoenberg-Bartók axis.

With this tide running strong, George Gershwin, completely aware that he was not in the contemporary trend, elected to be George Gershwin and thereby made one of the major contributions of his time.

What is the nature of a modern romantic or of the romantic concept? The term was born of an eighteenth- and early-nineteenth-century revolt against the political, religious, and artistic principles associated with rigid neo-classicism. In the arts and in literature it was characterized by a new liberalism in form and subject matter and encouraged emphasis on aesthetic feeling and originality. This resulted in new schools based on nature and the more simple values; revived interest in medieval tales, lyric poems, and so on. Possibly its greatest champion was

Rousseau and in France the movement produced Chateaubriand, Victor Hugo, Lamartine, Théophile Gautier, George Sand, and Balzac. The movement spread to England, and Shelley, Keats, Bulwer-Lytton, Dickens, Byron, Stevenson, and many others comprise the English romantic group.

Germany's response was Goethe, Schiller, Kleist, Grimm, Schopenhauer, to name but a small number of the complete contingent.

Best Americans associated with the romantic tendencies were Hawthorne, Edgar Allan Poe, Cooper, and Melville.

It is difficult to fix romanticism in art, but the list would most certainly include Géricault and Delacroix, while in music one must mention Berlioz, Schubert, and Schumann, and of course Wagner.

Then, for approximately fifty years, romanticism was dormant. When George Gershwin calls himself a "modern romantic," it does not mean that his music fits this former romantic pattern, although the underlying principles, as in his works of glamorous and fantastic explorations, the beauty in the lives of simple or native people, his verve and spirit, carry with them the same essential romantic spirit. But to this romantic concept he introduced elements and mutations hitherto unknown to it. His was the age of the skyscraper, the motor car, the express train, the airplane. These elements became, and very naturally, one of his points of departure; the essence of his inventions.

Romanticism is seen in a new light today and it gives philosophical verisimilitude to George Gershwin's choice of direction. Says Paul Tillich, one of our most advanced and distinguished philosophers: "Not conformity but differentiation is the end of the ways of God. Self-affirmation of one's uniqueness and acceptance of the demands of one's individual nature are the right courage to be." And again: "The pragmatist philosophers are not always aware of the fact that courage to create implies the courage to replace the old by the new—the new for which there are no norms and criteria; the new which is a risk and which, measured by the old, is incalculable."

In expressing individualistic courage, and tracing the relationship that extends in the romantic and naturalistic forms, Paul Tillich finds that the courage to be one's self has been brought to the most powerful expression in the existentialist movement. He makes here a point that most exactly covers the case of George Gershwin: "The courage to be as oneself is never completely separated from the other pole, the courage to be as a part; and even more, that overcoming isolation and facing the danger of losing one's world in the self-affirmation of oneself as an individual are a way toward something which transcends both self and world." George Gershwin, young as he was, most certainly transcended both himself and the world.

There seems to be but one valid distinction between the classic and the romantic artist: their separate attitudes toward reality. As De Schloezer succinctly puts it:

The art of the first [classic] is a closed world and the art of the second [romantic] is wide open to life. . . . The romantic tries to act on reality and succeeds. He is "realist" in the very sense that we call the classicist "anti-realist," he welcomes life in his art. Since art is synonymous with artifice, he has to impose certain conventions but he tries to reduce them to a minimum. Hence his ceaseless strife against the rules, his thirst for liberty, which liberty he has to have in order to give his art authenticity, i.e., bring his work nearer to the diverse, multiform, unstable, fugitive reality. The romantic wants to spread out, to abolish the frontiers, to bring in alien elements.

In short, the romanticist, in this case George Gershwin, wants to create the beauty which is the reward of adventurousness. Everything George wrote, to a degree, is full of contrasting cadences of a dynamic and strongly individual quality; his syncopation and the exploitation of concurrent and apparently irreconcilable rhythms are at first exasperating "and eventually exciting." He brought us back to a world of music, brimming with natural, romantic vitality. As Gilbert Seldes wrote: "One had forgotten that there still existed in the world a force so boundless, an exaltation so high, that anyone could storm heaven with laughter and cheers."

And George Gershwin had a passport. Stravinsky has said that every artist, no matter how far he may transcend every frontier, must have a passport, a nationalistic point of departure. George Gershwin had an *American* passport.

Porgy and Bess demands separate consideration. While its orchestration presents difficulties comparable to that imposed by Richard Strauss, and seems overcomplicated, it is nevertheless more expert than any of its predecessors among Gershwin works. The score of *Porgy and Bess* brims with rhythmic vitality. Gershwin's use of well-defined choral pattern with its attendant pounding rhythm achieves a primitive intensity without actually resorting to Negro melodies or spirituals. So close are these to the cries of the black man that they seem to have a common origin.

Porgy and Bess did not fit the pattern of opera as an art form hundreds of years old. Thirty years of my life were spent in managing and directing grand opera, ballet, and concert performances and performers. Grand opera never convinced me. It is a group of components divided against themselves. Opera scores are necessarily arbitrary and often stylized, but the librettos almost universally mirror some banal interlude. The acting is stilted, unnatural, and ludicrous. The settings and costumes, although there are remarkable exceptions, are usually unimaginative attempts at realism, stone castles which ripple at the touch of an awkward chorus member. A vulgar conspiracy aimed at seducing simultaneously all the senses, opera seldom transcends its obvious limitations.

True, there have been performances in my experience, those rare occasions when the scenery and lighting were in the hands of artists, the orchestra directed by an inspired despot, a chorus trained to perfection, and stars singing at their animal best, when the entire ensemble metamorphosed itself into a homogeneous attack and hypnotized an audience. These are rare occasions.

The truth is that opera, developed as an extravagant diversion for kings, emperors, and czars, is false as an art form. The pleasure or the satisfaction or the excitement which held me for so many years had nothing to do with the performances themselves, as theatrical experience. Instead, there was the challenge of trying to make such a preposterous assortment of unrelated elements ever come to fruition as an opera performance, a considerable feat.

The recipe: You begin with money, say a million dollars. Take a group of very solvent guarantors or members of a financially strong board. These men must be animated by unselfish motives, or at least want to see their names on programs and in publications as art patrons. Their wives will inspire them to be civic minded, their imaginations running riot with thoughts of what the couturiers will do with their evening gowns, and the jewels that will be given a breather from the vault. Take a group of young, ambitious youngsters who want

G. G. by Covarrubias

a musical career as the basis of your chorus. Or if you are in the very largest cities, you will find a group of trained veterans whose gray hair attests to the fact that they had no ambitions beyond the weekly chorus pay check. Take the nearest available theatrical scenery provider and either take his stock ensembles, or bring in a recommended scenery painter who will turn out productions to fit your repertoires. Take an ambitious and strong-willed conductor who will be able to whip into shape the chorus, the ballet, the orchestra, and the assorted stars, and give a performance on a minimum of rehearsals. Rehearsals can ruin you because of the staggering stagehand bill and other like expenses for an opera that will be given but once, or a few times, during your season. Take the great names among sopranos, tenors, baritones, and contraltos, the greater the name the greater the box office, and the greater the box office, the greater the star's fee. Take a group of society women who have as great a sense of personal publicity as the stars and organize them into a committee to work for the success of your season with balls, teas, committee meetings, and other promotional devices. Take a high-powered publicity agency who will guarantee that columns of stories and pictures will appear at the appropriate time everywhere. Take a theater or opera house that will hold hundreds of people, regardless of the acoustics of the place, as you must make some sort of a showing against the certain deficit. Take all the prima donnas who insist on top billing, on certain dressing rooms, on the conductor taking their arias at a certain tempo, and who will also insist that the tenor will not be so great that he will overshadow her. Take all the tenors who will insist on top billing, on certain dressing rooms, on the conductors taking their arias at a certain tempo, and who will also insist that the soprano will not be so great that she will overshadow him. Same for contraltos and baritones.

Take opera patrons who will insist on having *their* seats the fourth row on the aisle, and next to Mrs. Plushbottom's party, or in the first stage box, or the Diamond Horseshoe, and who will want the privilege of returning their tickets for cash if something comes up at the last minute that prevents them from coming. Take a whole phalanx of husbands, gentlemen who love poker, *South Pacific,* and a chorus of beauties, put them in stiff formal attire, invite them to dinner parties preceding the opera performances so that they can arrive at a disturbingly late hour, and be generous and understanding as they reconsider the business deal they made that day while Jeritza is singing piteously to the sinister Scarpia. Take your conductor who threatens, ten minutes before curtain time, to walk out unless such-and-such conditions are immediately remedied. Take a good stormy night which delays streetcars, busses, limousines, and taxicabs. Take enough whiskey straight and aspirin to get you through a hideously chaotic evening, and you have had the joy of accomplishment in the worldly realm of art!

Porgy and Bess was a Theatre Guild production and, as such, took its chance with public favor, no guarantors, no imposing board of directors, no society backing.

Its libretto unfolded a story quite unfamiliar to the public and critics, a story of ignorant Negroes in a sordid environment. The cast was Negro. And, as a final argument against its acceptance by the fashionable world, the conventional-minded critics, and the opera-minded public, the music was based on jazz.

The composer was not a European. He was not known as a composer of *really* serious music, despite the success of his symphonic works. He was not "accepted" in the world of serious musicians and serious music.

The fact that he was a fabulous success as a *theater* composer reacted against him in most circles. He would have had a much easier path had he been completely unknown. He was indeed *too* well known. How could a graduate of Tin Pan Alley and a composer of light, *trivial* music write a grand opera? The whole idea was absurd. And what indeed was jazz? A crazy, more or less erotic fad, a music that appealed to the baser instincts, a movement that came from our commonest soil, a stimulant to man's lower passions.

In the light of what has happened, these ideas, so prevalent at the time, seem prejudiced and uninformed. But they were the current attitudes, as well I can attest.

What I saw and heard at the first performance of *Porgy and Bess* was a music drama stripped of every artificiality of the operatic convention. There were no stilted recitatives; no interpolated ballets, unrelated to the libretto; no grandiose scenery; no jewel- and fur-laden costumes; no contrived effects that gave a prima donna or a tenor an opportunity for vocal pyrotechnics; no chorus which came and departed when the performance needed a change of pace; no music composed to sweep audiences off their feet into an emotional never-never-land.

Here was a story of primitive people breathing, singing, working, playing, and *living*. Here was music which did not break with the story, but gave it continuity; music with elements that audiences instantly recognized as valid expression of contemporary mores; music of profound emotional content encased in convincing aesthetic form.

The performance had a coherence as precise as that of Mozart, and a freedom that pulsated with life. And here, for the first time, I heard, not an old master creation reeking of another day, but a slice right out of the contemporary world of our American South. Giving verisimilitude to the entire concept was the inventive beat of jazz, jazz dedicated to, and fully demonstrating its validity as, a sound musical form.

3. The Man

IT WAS a cloudless afternoon; the gentle breeze was heavy with the scent of orange blossoms. Water in the swimming pool was very blue. I lay there in the sun looking at a gray stucco house on Roxbury Drive. George Gershwin had made that Beverly Hills house distinguished. After he came to Hollywood for a picture with Fred Astaire, the industry, dimly realizing George's potentiality, would not let him go.

The richness of the Gershwin environment was remarkable. His home was always full of friends, and their talk and laughter were very much part of the scene. Dinner or lunch included, in addition to Leonore and Ira, a group of whatever friends were in the house, in the swimming pool, or on the tennis court. It was a convivial atmosphere, full of talk, lashed with argument and wit, and usually charged also with a special sardonic humor provided by the peripatetic Oscar Levant.

But there always was a contradiction in all this. Certainly the house, the grounds, the whole ensemble of Gershwin artifacts contributed to a misleading impression. The endless conversations of the friends who had dropped in for a swim, for cocktails, or friendly talk, also gave the general impression of just another wealthy Beverly Hills place, home of a family devoted strictly to leisure which liked to entertain very informally. Such an impression could hardly have been more false. The swimming pool and the tennis court were actively employed, but the people there were producers or actors or writers, carrying on the necessities of their professions, exchanging ideas that would produce results on a national or world scale. And George and Ira themselves were seldom, if ever, idle.

To list celebrities is boring, but my readers can be certain that almost every day many of them made personal appearances at the Gershwin continuous party. Harold Arlen, Yip Harburg, Moss Hart, George Pallay, Lillian Hellman, Arthur Kober, Edward G. Robinson were a few of the many.

Paulette Goddard and George seemed to be very attracted to each other. Paulette would emerge from her cabana in the scantiest of bathing suits and lie à la Cleopatra along the side of the pool. As she stretched out a languid hand to ruffle the hair of the swimming George, the anatomical display was superb. But she could be a charmer in other ways. Coming upon my Stravinsky book in George's library, she insisted on purchasing everything I had done that was in print—a very fetching compliment, indeed. Somewhere in this merry-go-round the young French actress Simone Simon played a part. Her specialty seemed to be the telephone. I have waited interminably for George to come from the phone, only to be told by him, "I was just talking to Simone." Simone temporarily changed the style of beauty in the eyes of Hollywood. Beauty at that time had been exemplified by Kay Francis, Joan Crawford, the Bennett sisters, and other more mature and sophisticated types. Along came Simone, adorable, cuddle-some, and Hollywood capitulated en masse. But that changed, too, in time.

Harold Arlen and Oscar Levant were also regular visitors; I never went to dinner at the Gershwin home when Oscar

Levant was not a guest. Arnold Schoenberg, that musical giant, came often for tennis. And there were Schoenberg and Gershwin with only a tennis net between them: two of the most discussed musicians alive. It was a sight I enjoyed, particularly with Albert Heink Sendrey, himself a musician. George, who had, as Sendrey said, made a respectable woman out of Jazz, opposed to that small, agile older man, who was beating new paths through the musical wilderness, paths that are now being explored by more and more musicians. Let Sendrey give his impressions:

There they were, those two contrasting giants of music, George Gershwin and Arnold Schoenberg, united in one common thought, to make a little ball scale the top of the net, as though nothing else mattered. Let shortsighted humanity sneer at dissonance—love-fifteen—let them call the *Rhapsody in Blue* a mere fad—fifteen-all—let them walk out grimacing and holding their ears —thirty-fifteen—let them say Tin Pan Alley, always Tin Pan Alley—forty-fifteen—so Boris Morros thinks *Verklaerte Nacht* would make a swell picture score? Forty-thirty—let them speak of *Porgy and Bess* as a musical dwarf, if it makes them happy. Game and set, six-two. "Hello, Al, glad to see you, do you mind waiting until Mr. Schoenberg has a chance to take his revenge? Thanks. Get yourself a drink, they are in a cooler beside the pool, and then come over and watch a real match. By the way, has Budge improved your game any?"

But get Schoenberg away from his tennis, and ask him about George, and here are some of the things you would hear: "Serious or not, George Gershwin is a composer, a man who lives in music, and expresses everything, serious or not, in music, because it is his native language. There are a number of 'serious' composers who learned to add notes together. But they are only serious because they lack humor. Beyond doubt that Gershwin was an innovator. What he has done with rhythm, harmony, and melody is not merely style. It is fundamentally different from the mannerism of many a serious composer. Such mannerism is based upon artificial presumptions, which are gained by speculation and are conclusions drawn from the fashions and aims current among contemporary composers at certain times. Such a style is a superficial union of devices applied to a minimum of idea, without any inner reason or cause. Such music could be taken to pieces and put together in a different way, and the result would be the same nothingness expressed by another mannerism. One could not do this with Gershwin's music. His melodies are not the products of a combination, nor of a mechanical union; but they are units and therefore could not be taken to pieces. Melody, harmony, and rhythm are not welded together, but cast. It is always one way with art—you get from a work about as much as you are able to give to it yourself."

Yes, in that beehive on North Roxbury Drive there were many things taking place that did not meet the eye, or the ear. Schoenberg spoke an entirely different musical language than did George, but Schoenberg was entirely aware that George spoke a true and new language, and that he spoke it extremely well.

When I arrived at the Gershwin residence it was my habit to slip upstairs, avoiding the crowd and the tumult. In a special room was George's easel, and George himself was usually there, painting away as though he were a thousand miles from pandemonium. As often as possible, he managed to get away for a few hours to paint. Asked if the gaiety below did not interfere with his painting, which he took very seriously, George replied, "Oh, no, it kind of stimulates me."

Shortly after he acquired his first work of art George began to paint. He took to painting with the same quality of gusto that he gave music, he reveled in it. He had the good fortune to enjoy the influence of Henry Botkin, who said that painting came remarkably natural to Gershwin. Without actually studying the technique of painting, Gershwin gladly accepted many pointers as well as encouragement from Botkin. He obviously plunged right in with considerable and laudable confidence, for even his earliest work, while comparatively crude, displayed a kind of definition not usual with the amateur.

All through his paintings there are treatments, forms, and manners reminiscent of his music. He was not modern, in the sense of Picasso or Braque, but he was in that solid middle ground that is occupied by such fine painters as Russell Cowles, Alexander Brook, and other contemporaries. And in every new picture you could discern growth and increased mastery. He had arrived at a proficiency surprising in one whose life was so crowded with internal and external events. He was certainly eclectic as a painter, but it was strength, not weakness. Technically, he was the peer of many men who have national reputations as painters. He was in love with color, and his palette in paint closely resembled the color of his music. Juxtapositions of greens, blues, sanguines, chromes, and grays fascinated him. He developed a very personal style of applying paint to canvas.

In the summer of 1957—at the home of Leonore and Ira Gershwin, we got out some of George's paintings, including the portrait of Arnold Schoenberg and a self-portrait, and it was good to see how well they stood up. George was working on the Schoenberg portrait at the time I was working on my Schoenberg book, and he actually hurried to finish his painting so that it could be included in the book, as it was.

One of the surprising talents George possessed was his bold, vital line in drawing. In 1932 he drew a portrait of Henry Botkin which has a lyrical quality reminiscent of Matisse, as does to a lesser extent his "Girl Reading," drawn in 1931. Probably his portraits are his best work. He painted his father, his mother, Jerome Kern, Dubose Heyward, and several of himself. His self-portrait at the easel is something of a *tour de force*. His portrait of Diego Rivera is superb.

One of his most exuberant paintings is a still life of "Orchids" in a vase painted in 1934. Here he applied paint with spirit and joy, in the manner of his friend Siqueiros, although without a trace of his friend's manner. One of my favorites is "Negro Sculpture," painted in 1934, a purely imaginative landscape with African sculpture in the foreground, while across the river a real native dance takes place against a background of palm forest. It has excellent feeling for color and rhythm.

Painting could have been a major factor in Gershwin's life, as it was one of his major interests. Reviewing an exhibition of his work after his death, Henry McBride wrote: "He was not yet actually great as a painter, but that was merely because he had not yet had the time—but he was distinctly on the way to that goal. He had all the aptitudes. If the soul be great, all the expressions emanating from that soul must be great."

As Botkin has said, George had an instinctive sense of art's creative processes and was especially sensitive to rhythm. I would add that he painted naturally with style, or, as I have said, he painted as he composed, which means he composed and painted entirely in his own happy manner. His music certainly influenced his painting and undoubtedly his painting would have eventually influenced his music.

Perhaps nothing about George Gershwin was more revealing than his collection of contemporary paintings. The first time I had an opportunity to see most of his major acquisitions in one group was in 1933. I was in Chicago to see Adolph Bolm, an old friend and associate; we had been together on the tours of the Diaghileff Ballet, and later I took Bolm's *Ballet Intime* on tour. We were entertained at the Chicago Art Club by the John Alden Carpenters. Bolm was working with this composer on ballets, either the *Skyscrapers*, or the *Krazy Kat* opus. After dinner Mrs. Carpenter led us toward the gallery where a really superlative collection of art was hanging, owned, she said, by George Gershwin. George's taste in art made a powerful impression on me. My hosts were happy to hear that it was art which had brought me in contact with Gershwin, and my story of our frequent meetings in New York galleries delighted them.

George loved his paintings, he understood them, he caressed them. There was great independence of judgment in his collecting, yet George's modern romanticism was ever present in his taste. We often talked about this quality which stamped his every activity and expression. He was pleased that this endowment could be discerned by others and often spoke about it as a *consistency* in his make-up. "If I were a poseur it would certainly show in both my painting and my music," he once remarked. And when I assured him that the modern romantic disposition was remarkably apparent in his collecting he was delighted. "I guess you can then call me monolithic in attitude," he replied.

George frequently came to my house to see and discuss my own collection. This had been a long time in the making. About 1916, I began placing something in a piggy bank every day. When $50.00 had been accumulated I made a payment on some long-desired work of art. Dealers seemed to be impressed with my prudent undertakings, as well as amused. The collection eventually grew at a more rapid pace as my affairs prospered, and came to consist of water colors, drawings, lithographs, and etchings by artists now very celebrated.

My visits to the George Gershwin house always increased my respect for *his* discernment. For instance, he had a very rare and choice Utrillo, not one of the Paris series of streets that demonstrate perspective, fine as they are, but a picture from the white period, about 1910, and painted in Brittany. It is a picture of museum quality and much more subtle than many of Utrillo's other works. It now hangs in the splendid new house Leonore and Ira have built in Beverly Hills, with several other fine pictures that were originally in George's group. His Modiglianis were superb. There were also an extremely stylized Derain of an early period when Derain was at his best; a fascinating Rousseau; and certainly one of the most impressive paintings in the entire output of Pascin. Another striking and very unusual picture that had attracted George was of a tall Negress, nude, by the American John Carroll. This picture has more strength than most characteristic paintings by Carroll. A Gauguin self-portrait again demonstrated George's perspicacity, and he loved the work of the iconoclast, Siqueiros, and had several of his pictures. The large composite picture of a concert hall that resembles a cross between Carnegie Hall and La Scala in Milan, in which the Gershwin family and friends are in the front rows, is a Siqueiros concoction. It was used on the title page of the George Gershwin book which, with the aid of many of George's friends and admirers, I produced in 1938.

Musicians are notoriously indifferent to any other art and this makes George's taste so exceptional as to be unique. Josef Stransky, the conductor of the New York Philharmonic, before its merger with the Damrosch organization, is the only other musician I know who had a sure sense about pictures, with the possible exception of Artur Rubinstein, the pianist.

Rouault fascinated George. My library of art books, especially Rouault, was in demand whenever he came to dinner, lunch, or just to talk. Rouault seemed to repel him at the same time, and he was endlessly curious as to why Rouault selected certain strong if not repulsive models and subjects. But he certainly understood and appreciated the Rouault painting technique, his heavy impasto, his magnificent sense of form, his bold treatment. George especially liked clowns, and later, as his own painting progressed, he came to a new understanding of the Rouault subject matter.

His examples of the work of painters always seemed to be unique. He owned a fine Max Weber, a Masson, and a good Léger. I recall a Thomas Benton, possibly a burlesque-theater scene, and was surprised and delighted that he owned a Kandinsky. In addition to some distinguished African sculpture, the portrait of George by Isamu Noguchi was one of the many first-class works of art in his home. Picasso's "The Absinthe Drinker," now in the Museum of Modern Art, the gift of J. H. Whitney, came from the Gershwin collection after George's death. There were few if any works, in a total of one hundred and forty, that were not outstanding from a strictly aesthetic standpoint.

It is clear that painting was something more than a hobby with George. There is a rich, revealing overtone in the art of painting that was very close to his own convictions and feeling about all art. We talked a great deal about the work of Paul Klee, of which I have many examples. George was just coming to Paul Klee, and his appreciation, intuitive perhaps, was keen. He studied some of my Klee water colors with a magnifying glass one day, then drew back and said, "What am I doing! My music would not stand up under that kind of scrutiny." In one of our last conversations about painting and artists, Gershwin said, "I know. It's very clear to me now. Picasso is the full symphony orchestra of painting, while Klee is a string quartet."

After our concerts were over and George had made a very generous gesture toward me in the settlement of costs not included in the original agreement, I carefully selected a Paul Klee water color from Galka Scheyer, who represented Klee in America, and gave it to him. Its subject matter was derived from the musical staff, clef, notes, and so forth, a very unusual and handsome work. George could have hardly been more demonstrative. A Rolls-Royce could not have meant more to him. Later I gave him one of my lithographs by Arthur B. Davies, another Romantic who is sure to come into vogue again; he is too exquisite to be lost in the dim past. George and I talked about the modernity of Davies, who had been one of the instigators of the now famous Armory Show.

After the death of George, perhaps six months elapsed, and then one day Ira appeared at my door. Going back to his car, he brought me the Klee water color I had given to George months before. "George loved this painting, and I know you loved it," he explained, "and I thought you should have it back." What a gracious and typical gesture from this admirable man.

In the stucco house on Roxbury Drive the inevitable Steinway occupied a corner of a huge living room. When George was at the piano he would reluctantly leave it to come to lunch or dinner. George loved aromatic pipe tobacco and fine cigars. Seldom was he without one or the other, and this aroma, added to the sparkling music and good conversations, provided the over-all atmosphere with a note of opulence that well fitted George's own enthusiasm, spirit, and generosity.

The Gershwin household had a personality and a quality not encountered elsewhere. Most of his guests felt like staying on forever, and that, I am sure, would have been all right with George. He loved his family and they loved him. His life and work were both sustained and inhibited thereby. Socially minded families allow for no privacy, and some of the Gershwins' early work was accomplished in the same room with poker games and talkative women.

Ira, his brother, was unquestionably the greatest pillar in George's life. Ira is a rare character. In his lyrics a witty, expert, arch, deeply understanding man, he receives the world as it comes. He makes few verbal judgments on people or things, although to know him is to respect his very well-ordered convictions. His modesty and loyalty are among the marvels of my acquaintance, and in these he has never changed under the stress of wealth, success, and all their concomitants.

Ira understood George. George depended on Ira. George was inspired by Ira and encouraged. It was a partnership, a brotherhood, and a teamwork of the rarest sort, as when they collaborated on *Of Thee I Sing,* a unique work in the American theater. When the beautiful and keen Leonore married Ira and began to take a hand in the Gershwin affairs, there was no break. She moved smoothly into the picture.

One thing writers seemed to have overlooked is the amount and the diverse character of George's work. In the history of music, probably no other composer has been called on for a parallel output. For instance, George, working on a serious passage of a new composition, would be called to the theater or the studio. A new sequence had been added to a musical comedy or a movie; it needed more music, now! George would immediately provide that music and it would be in-

Drawing of Leonore by G. G.

corporated in rough manuscript. This went on year after year. From work on the *Concerto,* or *Second Rhapsody*, he would turn to numbers for *Of Thee I Sing*. Conventionally, a composer has pursued somewhat of a straight line of music in one category, so to speak. George ricocheted from one *quality* of task to another, and from the intimacy of his own living room to the chaos of rehearsal stage.

George was always the recipient of a great deal of good-natured and sometimes astringent comment because of his continuous preoccupation with music. George S. Kaufman's gentle remark, "I'd bet on George any time—in a hundred-yard dash to the piano," and Oscar Levant's acid question, "Tell me, George, if you had to do it all over again—would you still fall in love with yourself?" are typical. But neither of these close friends really meant this witty spoofing. Bennett Cerf came much closer to the truth when he observed: "I have never seen a man happier, more bursting with the sheer joy of living, than George was when he was playing his songs."

Increasingly people and events were adding their major and minor voices to the growing Gershwin prestige. A significant fragment appears in Sir Osbert Sitwell's *Laughter in the Next Room:* "Though Gershwin was not an intimate friend of mine, I knew him and liked him, and he would usually come to have luncheon with us when he visited London. He possessed a fine racial appearance: nobody could have mistaken him for anyone but a Jew. Tall and vigorous, his clearly cut face with its handsome ram's head, the features prominent, but, as it were, streamlined, indicated will power, character, and talent. I have always understood that he was the son of immigrants from Russia or Germany and was brought up in the poorest quarter of New York: but his manners were notably excellent, his voice was pleasant, and though the force of his personality was plain in his whole air, he was modest in bearing, and I never noticed in him a trace of the arrogance with which he has been credited. Many of his contemporaries, it may be, attributed an exaggerated value to his celebrated *Rhapsody in Blue,* but at least the hundreds of songs and dances he wrote were altogether typical in their audacity of the age that gave them birth; the twenties lived and expired to his ingenious tunes, so expert of their kind, and no chronicle on the epoch could fail to mention them and their pervasive influence; since they were as symptomatic of the triple capitals of the Insouciant Decade as Johann Strauss was of early Franz Josef Vienna, or Offenbach in the sixties."

Proof of George's modesty was his interest and devotion to *all* music. He was an exceptionally informed man. His love for and knowledge of the chamber music of Mozart, Brahms, and Debussy, his deep feeling for the Mozart operas, are examples. He was familiar with almost everything written by Bach and Beethoven. He had explored the world of Rameau, Pergolesi, Palestrina, and Gluck. But the greatest masters were like *old masters* hanging in a museum. Full of admiration for them, he was nevertheless going in another direction, his direction. And while grateful for the rich heritage from Palestrina to Bartók, and very excited about the men of his time, Schoenberg, Ravel, Milhaud, Hindemith, Berg, Stravinsky, he knew he belonged in still another world. But his interest in Berg, for instance, was so serious that he took time from his own heavy schedule to go to the *Wozzeck* performance in Philadelphia.

And he studied with Schoenberg. Even before he knew Schoenberg personally, he had provided a fund so that several talented Americans could study with this master when he came from Europe to teach in Boston. When both Gershwin and Schoenberg found themselves in Los Angeles, there was an immediate association, extremely profitable to both.

The more music George explored and grew to love the more certain he felt of his own direction. There was no jealousy in Gershwin nor was there any temptation to be influenced. This is a very singular condition in the world of creative men.

One of the significant aspects of his mind and attitude was his insistence on knowing the basic rules, whether in composing or in painting. Then he would proceed to work out his own rules, often in direct opposition to standard procedure or established formulas.

Early in his career George encountered an important man who helped lay the foundations of his musical understanding. For many months Gershwin took two piano lessons a week from Edward Kilenyi, a most sympathetic teacher. Later, at George's suggestion, Kilenyi engaged orchestral players to come and explain, and play, each instrument in the orchestra. This invaluable experience enabled George to grasp the meaning as well as the *possibilities* of each instrument. When George began his larger works, he had an excellent knowledge of how far he could push his ideas within the compass of the conventional orchestra. In later years he showed many players latent or unsuspected powers of instruments they had played for years. Only a few conductors and not many composers have been so informed and armed.

Southern California, and in fact the whole West, had been very good to me. All my concert projects had flourished, and I had helped to establish opera on the coast. The West was a fast-growing, dynamic, new world. Opera had proved to be just what Western society needed as a great annual festival, with all its adjuncts of dinner parties, beautiful clothes, jewels: an expression of its enormous prosperity.

But the arrival of George and Ira Gershwin immediately suggested to me that performances of Gershwin music with George participating would be especially appreciated by the younger crowd which was not particularly interested in oper-atic performances. I gave a luncheon for the critics of all the Los Angeles newspapers and magazines for the purpose of disclosing my Gershwin plans, asking their advice and co-operation. Because I had been continuously shuttling back and forth across the continent and spending several months each year in New York I was as familiar with the events, the mores, and the thinking in New York as I was aware of the Los Angeles picture. Or I thought I was, until this luncheon, which was quite an experience. These critics were all close friends of mine and we could and did express ourselves freely. They had nothing but discouragement for my plan of a pair of Gershwin concerts. "We know that Gershwin is a bril-liant young musician, but he is not well enough known here in the West, and there is not enough substance to his music to make two entire evening concerts palatable. People just won't go for a full program of jazz."

Nevertheless, early in October 1936 I wrote George a letter proposing a couple of concerts using the Philharmonic Orchestra of Los Angeles, which at that time was one of the best orchestras in the country. The orchestra management each year engaged the men on individual contracts for a cer-tain number of engagements. I was aware, being an adviser to the management, that not enough concerts had been booked in southern California to absorb the players' contracts. There-fore, when I proposed to engage the entire organization for two concerts outside the regular subscription season, the management was delighted.

On October 13, 1936, I received a reply from George assuring me of his interest in such a project and asking me to telephone him. On October 23 I received another letter from him, thanking me for some books and reiterating his interest in the concerts. In fact, he had, in anticipation, inspected both the Shrine and the Philharmonic auditoriums, the two possible places where a Gershwin concert could be held. His enthusiasm for the project was obviously great.

We planned to hold our concerts early in February of the following year, 1937. We engaged Alexander Smallens to conduct the *Rhapsody in Blue* and the *Concerto in F*, with George to be piano soloist with each. Then George said he would conduct the *Cuban Overture*. Later, as our enthusiam grew, we engaged a Negro chorus and added some numbers from *Porgy and Bess*, with George conducting. We also decided to use the Philharmonic Auditorium, which I managed, in preference to the Shrine. Doing two concerts in the Philharmonic, which seats approximately 3,000 persons, seemed more advantageous than using the Shrine, which seats 6,400, and is apt to seem huge for anything short of *Turandot* or *Tristan und Isolde*. Finally we selected the dates, February 10 and 11, 1937.

For these concerts I designed a very special George Gershwin program, printed with horizontal lines between the lines of type, a rather stunning piece in red and blue on a heavy white paper. These programs proved so popular that our patrons took all they could find, and came back for more. The result is that I have but one single copy.

As preparations for the concerts proceeded there were a multitude of details to be handled. George and I went often to the Negro district in Central Avenue to pick our chorus members through auditions. Finally we had selected approximately thirty young men and women with glorious voices, and training began. George undertook to train the chorus, but his heavy schedule at the studio (he was at RKO working on a Fred Astaire-Ginger Rogers movie) caused him to turn over a great part of the training to our friend Alexander Steinert. Nevertheless, those trips back and forth from my house to his house, to the Philharmonic Auditorium, to Central Avenue will remain some of my most treasured memories. George had a new Cord car, a front-drive vehicle of great chic, one of the earliest streamlined cars. He loved to drive it. My interest, though, was in his conversation, for Los Angeles being a huge sprawling community we spent hours in crossing town to our various engagements.

George and I talked art. Or we talked music. One of the things we discussed was the string quartet on which he was working at the time. This was a fascinating subject, as the quartets of Beethoven, of Haydn, Debussy, and Ravel were among my favorites. He talked of the form his quartet would take, a fast opening movement, followed by a very slow second movement, based on themes he had heard when visiting Folly Island off the Carolina coast with DuBose Heyward. The sounds of the dominant themes were so insistent that he had not bothered to write them down. "It's going through my head all the time," George said, "and as soon as I have finished scoring the next picture, I'm going to rent me a little cabin up in Coldwater Canyon, away from Hollywood, and get the thing down on paper. It's about to drive me crazy, it's so damned full of new ideas!"

George had very sound and definite convictions. In our Cord-car conversations we covered the water front. Machine-age America, he believed, had influenced form less than it had tempo, speed, and sound, but from these new attitudes and influences would eventually come new *forms*. When I called his attention to the fact that indeed *Porgy and Bess* was a *new form*, he did not deny it, but quickly changed back to a more impersonal conversation; this was partly his innate modesty, and partly because he believed that *Porgy and Bess* might have come too early as far as the critics were concerned. He spoke at length on the new sounds and instruments that had appeared, of how he used four taxi horns for an effect in *An American in Paris*, of how George Antheil used everything, including airplane propellers, doorbells, typewriter keys, and such, and of Honegger's use of the steam-engine exhaust rhythms and pulsations in *Pacific N° 231*. We both agreed that this "lifting" of noises and the employment of new instruments, or machines *as* instruments, were of course superficial and a little too direct. But they did indicate a willingness to enlarge horizons. I spoke of the Stravinsky *Rites of Spring* as a work where the overtones of the machine age and the primitive rites of the soil were employed *once removed*, rather than in direct application: George not only agreed, but said that this work had exercised a very great influence on him, although it did not color his work which, as he so simply expressed it, "is just me." But the more profound things that George said during these talks were his credo. He was certain that various tonalities and sounds, no matter how exotic, strange, or seemingly significant, mean nothing unless they grow out of ideas and musical convictions. Music is made, he said, of *ideas and feeling*.

He believed it was impossible for the public to assimilate real greatness quickly. Mechanism and feeling, he believed, must go hand in hand. He cited the case of a skyscraper as a triumph of the machine, and a great emotional experience, its mass and proportions the result of both emotion and calculation. To those who refused to see the power and the vitality of jazz, or even refused to call it music, George had a witty answer: Jazz *is* music, it uses the same notes that Bach used. It was pretty conclusive. He believed jazz to be an American achievement, because it came from the heart, and he believed it would endure.

He was especially articulate about the possibility of music being heard by millions through recordings, radio, and movies. Music, he said, was made to be heard, and anything that allowed more people to hear it, benefited people as well as the composer. He was aware that methods of reproduction can also distort and be harmful, but he believed that people, through hearing, would slowly learn to criticize and evaluate.

One thing on which we agreed with vehemence was that there was no such thing, as European critics are wont to say, as machine-made music. The machine is merely the reproducer and the distributor of music; music itself must always be the product of the human heart, soul, and hand.

George Gershwin was proud that he was an American. When he said, "My people are American, my time is today, music must repeat the thought and aspirations of the times," he was simply giving utterances to a quality inherent in his music. He believed one could express pride in America without appearing either presumptuous or naïve. He was aware of this country's scope, of its vastness, and had an appreciation of its vitality, an understanding of its tremendous destiny.

In every way the United States is big. There is no pettiness in America's contours, whether natural or man-made. This has had its effect upon our people; it creates one of the subtle but profound differences between the American and the

European. We may be, and sometimes are, crude and immature; but we are a big, a vital people, fortunately removed from the suspicions and rancors of a more disillusioned Europe.

Not all the conversations George and I had were serious. He talked often of the antics of the boys and girls being trained for our concert; it was an enormous event for them, their first time on a stage.

George often spoke about how fortunate he had been in obtaining Rouben Mamoulian to direct the first *Porgy and Bess* performances, a question given priority by me when it became my turn later to produce this music drama. Mamoulian, in George's mind, was ideal. Mamoulian had staged the production of *Porgy*, the play, and, what was most important, Mamoulian, through his experiences at the Eastman Theatre, knew opera. He had been able to bring his knowledge of both to the new form. George's great appreciation, too, of Ann Brown and Todd Duncan was very touching; and he had a great admiration of Bubbles as Sportin' Life. Hearing him talk, one would believe that George held them quite as responsible as he for the way people loved *Porgy and Bess*.

Remembering the critics' attitude we did not take any chances on selling out the two performances; we formed a Committee of Young Men, headed by my friend Durward Howes, himself a young man of accomplishment. Preceding the concerts, this committee gave a reception for George at the Hollywood-Plaza Hotel. There George met about three hundred young men of southern California, all about his age. He had a wonderful time, because there was a piano in the ballroom.

The concerts, of course, were remarkable. Hundreds were turned away for lack of seats at each performance. As a matter

Caricature of Ira by G. G.

of fact we were sold out a week before the concerts and had to return checks for seats from all over the West. One can even use that tattered word "sensational" to describe our success. At rehearsals Smallens seemed to be inspired, and George beamed and played with a special *élan*. One day after rehearsal I congratulated George on his mastery of the players. "You have perfect discipline, and that is rare with this bunch," I had told him. George replied quietly, "Sure, they know I'm not a phony."

At the second concert, unknown to a single person in the audience, George had suffered a black-out while playing the *Concerto in F*. He said afterward that everything suddenly went black and he missed a few bars. Smallens covered this nicely. George regained complete control and continued the performance brilliantly.

Following the concert, we gave a big party at one of the fashionable night spots on the Sunset Strip. George was in great spirits, and the whole group, exclusively celebrities, seemed to have been electrified by what they had heard. As he chatted with me, Jack Benny, the old maestro, said, "Armitage, you have a lot of nerve, this thing was too damn good for Hollywood." Dining with George, Ira, and a few of their friends, our enthusiasm running high, I proposed that the next year we do *Porgy and Bess* on the coast, and take it across the country for a second New York engagement. George tempered his enthusiasm by a word of caution. "It's devilishly expensive, Merle. The Theatre Guild lost money. Do you dare?" My reply was positive, possibly more positive than my reservations warranted, but I have always been happy that I burned my bridges and took a flying leap into fate. "We can do it, George, because the capacity of our theaters is greater than those in New York, at least a third more." This seemed to satisfy him, for he replied with one of his characteristic smiles, "I guess you know what you are doing."

The night before I departed for Europe in 1937 I had dinner at the Gershwin ménage. "You know my taste and I trust your judgment," George said, standing beside my car when I left. "If you find anything that belongs in my collection, cable me the price. I am especially interested in a Kokoschka."

Those were the last words I heard George Gershwin speak, except for his cheery "Good-by."

4. The Critics

IN COLLECTING art, I had begun with the most established and classical of artists. When you are young and inexperienced, lacking a frame of reference, you must feel sure of your course. Modern art was unknown to me then, and in ten years' time my little collection contained Rembrandts, Goyas, Whistlers, Redons, among Europeans, and such contemporaries as Bellows, Kent, Davies, and Carroll. It was a good start, and my collecting became a major interest.

One afternoon I went to the Metropolitan Museum to see a joint show of the work of Paul Gauguin and Vincent Van Gogh. Apparently these men were as strange and vaguely known to the public as they were to me, for the huge galleries were almost empty. But that afternoon is a historical moment in my life. Here were a sense of freedom, a boldness, a use of brilliant color that hypnotized me. Some of those pictures, Van Gogh's "Self-portrait," "The Postman," "Crows over the Wheat Field," the "Portrait of Dr. Gachet," and "Bedroom at Arles," remain as fresh in my memory as if I had seen them yesterday. In the works of Gauguin, particularly the Tahitian paintings, I sensed an aura of eroticism that was fascinating.

It was a turning point. I have never lost my interest and my love for old masters, particularly the Italian, Flemish, and French primitives. Piero Della Francesca, Giotto, Mantegna, Botticelli, Dürer, Blake, and El Greco especially, are, and always will be, great experiences. But as I began to explore the works of my contemporaries and came to know Picasso, Braque, Klee, Matisse, Cézanne, and Rouault, these moderns brought me a sense of excitement and vigor which I particularly understood as of my time and environment. They paralleled the other new forces taking over the world.

In seeking the answer to the difficulty Gershwin was having with the critics, and remembering my own experience with modern art, I began a private search and inquiry into the experience of all artists and composers, or possibly an examination of what had happened to various new "movements," in the past two hundred years or more.

During my research for the Stravinsky book which was published in 1936, I had come upon some hard-to-believe reviews printed in Mozart's time. They were in journals brought to America by German refugees with whom I have lost contact, otherwise I would quote them verbatim. But in substance they advised the young master to "give up this vulgar dissonance, and return to harmony." This, about Mozart, the great disciple of lucidity and purity!

As I dug into contemporary opinions expressed so freely about both painters and composers, the whole pattern began to take shape. Any innovator meets an almost solid phalanx of opposition, misunderstanding, and ridicule. Judgments are made solely, or almost exclusively, on the basis of past and accepted forms and formulas.

Of course the attitude of the critic is very human and very understandable. Everything and anything new and without precedent tears or damages his frame of reference. He has everything catalogued in his mind, everything in its place. Past innovations appear only as a part of the pattern, as he views it in his panorama of the past. He has no place, in this pattern, for new figures that do not fit into the established scheme, and he therefore rejects them subconsciously, and he fights them consciously. They are odd shapes, they don't belong, and he can prove this by unveiling for you the whole history of music or art neatly fitted together like a mosaic.

Not until the new has itself become a recognizable pattern, accepted and approved, will he be able to see *how* and *where* this segment of component will fit into the over-all scheme. And of course with every generation, as new forms are created, tested, and finally accepted, this grand scheme is continually subjected to this, for critics, painful evolution and reconstruction.

Everyone is familiar with the classic case of Bach who supported his family of approximately twenty children by working as a church organist. It was not until more than a half-century later that Mendelssohn brought to the world's attention the glories of Bach's creative immensity. Less well known is the experience of Giovanni Palestrina, who, having written some of the most sublime and timeless music, supported himself by employment as choirmaster at the Vatican (1551) and in churches of Rome. G. Battista Pergolesi (1710–36) had to wait until our time for a full recognition of his great contribution to musical literature.

At the turn of the century, Debussy was approaching the maturity of his powers. Here is a malicious, if humorous, paragraph written by Jean Lorrain in a Paris journal, dated January 4, 1904. It expressed much of the contemporary feeling about Debussy and is indeed a gem:

Just as *they* were convulsed with admiration over the sunny *pizzicati* of that little masterpiece *L'Après-Midi d'un Faune,* they have now declared that we must go into raptures over the deliberate dissonances of the lengthy recitatives of *Pelléas* [*Pelléas et Mélisande*]. Those long-drawn chords and those perpetual beginnings of repeatedly announced phrases have an enervating effect. A kind of titillation that is at first pleasurable, then exasperating, and, in the end, cruelly painful, is inflicted on the ears of the audience by the continual repetition of a theme that is constantly interrupted and which never terminates. This work with its limbo-like atmosphere and its occasional little shocks so very artistic (oh, my dear!) and so upsetting (you can imagine!) received the united votes of a public consisting of snobs and poseurs.

Within ten years Paris was the scene of a production greeted with a similar embarrassing and an even more hostile reception. Diaghileff came to town with Stravinsky's *Le Sacre du Printemps*. As Arnold L. Haskell tells it:

The new theatre [Les Champs-Elysées] could have received no finer advertisement than the outcry that followed upon the production of *Le Sacre*. Its details have become too well known to need repetition. The music was of a kind unheard before, the smart crowd behaved like hooligans, and pandemonium was let loose. Stravinsky, in the wings, hung on to the frantic Nijinsky's coat collar to prevent him rushing on the stage, while Diaghileff, in a frenzy, ordered the lights first off, and then on, and Astruc [theater manager] shouted, "First listen, then hiss." The Dowager Comtesse de Pourtalès informed Astuc, as she swept out, that if he repeated such foolishness it was the last time she would be seen in his theater.

Strange, almost incredible, reading, now.
As Boris de Schloezer admonishes us:

And who guarantees us against the insurgence of some great composer who will turn the lot of these traditions bottom side up? One may be sure that in such a contingency, people will not fail to object to this "new movement"; and against this "revolutionary" stuff they will set the *true tradition;* but since the musician of genius will, in spite of all this, impose himself, they will end by annexing him, and by discovering that although he *innovates* it is "nevertheless undeniable that he" connects with the above-mentioned *tradition* and that he is only developing it and enriching it. Such, in short, was the story of Debussy, at first rejected as *against clear ideas, contrary to the Latin genius,* and so forth and today, quite rightly, considered the French musician *par excellence.*

Nor are the critics and the public the sole proprietors of the hydraulic brakes and the reverse gear. Indeed, the public has sometimes understood values not sensed by the intellectuals. Often the artist himself is the first to condemn a revolution not of his own making. Jean Cocteau writes:

An artist can expect no help from his peers. Any form which is not *his* must be unbearable to him and upset him at the outset. I have seen Claude Debussy sick at orchestra rehearsals of Stravinsky's *Le Sacre du Printemps.* He was discovering the beauty of that music. The form he had given to his soul suffered from another form which did not match it. Whence will the help come? From no one. And that is when art begins to use obscure maneuvers of nature in a reign opposed to it, which even seems to fight it, or turn its back.

Years ago I visited Frank Lloyd Wright in Arizona where a crew of draftsmen were polishing the construction details of a now-famous structure. Three days of friendly hospitality. Every evening Wright held forth in his impressive, pontifical manner on life and art and particularly architecture. On my last evening, presenting the master with an album of Debussy records, I touched off the fireworks. "Don't you know, young man, that no music has been written since Mozart? How dare you inflict this pseudo-stuff on me?" he exploded. I replied that it was embarrassing that one of my most admired geniuses had not been able to understand men in other fields who had fought the good fight and had achieved quite as much as had he. "I could as easily maintain," I continued, "that the man who first erected four stone walls, and placed a roof over them, had said all there was to say about architecture." It made the point, and the subject was changed. Wright, however, held no rancor. Some months later his *Autobiography* was published and the copy he sent was autographed, "To my friend Merle Armitage, a good fellow in the desert, with my admiration."

The art of painting has met similar stupidity, ridicule, and opposition. In 1934 John Hemming Fry wrote a book entitled *The Revolt Against Beauty*. Here is one of its paragraphs:

... the clumsy daubs of Cézanne, the stupid, half-baked struggles of Van Gogh, the vulgar dropsical malformations of Gauguin, and later the psychopathic mutilations of Matisse, Picasso, and their followers.... Do you object? Are not ugliness, vulgarity, sadistic deformation, and obscenity human attributes? Have not these as much claim to be the subjects of representation in painting as the virtues and beautiful figures, poetry, and grandeur? But, so are syphilis and cancer attributes of the human being; then why not encourage the spread of syphilis and cancer? Certainly no man or woman of normal mental health would be attracted by the sadistic obscene deformations in the paintings of Cézanne, Modigliani, Matisse, Gauguin, and the other Fauves.

This was written at the time George Gershwin's works were being submitted to the evaluations of the music critics.

But let me quote further, from the men then informing the

public through newspapers, magazines, and books as to what was what in the world of art. Thomas Craven, a man with enough reputation to appear in *Scribner's* magazine, is quoted in one of his sallies of 1938. "The art of Impressionism . . . a photostatic method of reproducing in paint the colors and tones of nature, a pleasant pastime that left the imagination unemployed."

Of Degas, Paul Mantz, writing in *Le Temps,* said: "Destined for a small place in the history of cruel arts." An unsigned article in the New York *Times* said in part, "Degas is repulsive, but he is not foolish like some." Of Manet, the celebrated Dante Gabriel Rossetti said, "There is a man named Manet, whose pictures are for the most part mere scrawls, and who seems to be one of the lights of the French School. Courbet, the head of it, is not much better." Of Claude Monet, the eminent Roger Ballu had this to say, "One must have seen the canvases of Cézanne and Monet to imagine what they are. They provoke laughter and are lamentable." Our own Royal Cortissoz, one of the arbiters of aesthetic taste in George Gershwin's time, said, "Cézanne was simply an offshoot of the impressionist school, who never quite learned his trade, and accordingly in his dealings with landscape, still life, and figure, was not accustomed to paint nonsense." Of the art of Gauguin, August Strindberg admitted, "I cannot grasp your art, and cannot like it." Matisse suffered this from Thomas Craven: "He is essentially a light talent, an ornamentalist whose designs are more applicable to silks, costumes, cretonnes, and ceramics than to pictorial space. His nimble fingers are closer to *La Vie Parisienne* than his inflated followers have even suspected."

It was open season, of course, when Rouault began to exhibit his monumental canvases. In a book published in 1914,

Gustave Coquiot said: "Corpulent scullery-wenches, Venuses from the sewer, they squatted like so many epileptic toads, or offered themselves up, their abdomens swelling and their adornment consisting of thicket-like manes of hair. This was not luxurious; it was debauched and putrid. It would have taken a monk to understand these nauseating works; one turned away and rushed towards the prettiness of M. d'Espagnat." Nor did Corot come off unscathed. Maurice de Vaines, writing contemporaneously in *Revue Nouvelle*, pontificated, "But where is the drawing, where the color, where is life and nature, where is anything whatsover, finally?" Van Gogh, of course, was an inviting target. There are books and articles that vilify him. But one quotation will exemplify the style and the content that reigned. Waldemar George, writing as late as 1933, made this immortal remark, "The work of Van Gogh is the work of a monomaniac." Even luscious Renoir, as healthy a painter as ever lived, had roadblocks such as this put in his path: "Just try to explain to M. Renoir that the torso of a woman is not a mass of decomposing flesh, its green and violet spots indicating the state of complete putrefaction of a corpse." Thomas Craven solved the riddle of Picasso with one trenchant statement: "His latest work . . . is the ghastliest claptrap ever bound in gold."

Reading these critical remarks today, it is difficult to realize such "critics" existed. Who were these men? Were they hack writers so feeble-minded that managing editors gave them what were considered the least important assignments? What were their capacities, background, and achievements that magazines and newspapers gave them employment? If they had been advising the public on financial matters, instead of art, many would certainly have ended in the penitentiary as swindlers. Not only were the judgments often false to the point of imbecility, but many of these statements prove their authors nasty-minded and more callous than peasants. Offensive!

The enlightened world has, of course, hailed every artist so grossly maligned in the remarks I have quoted. Indeed many of them produced pictures of such superb quality that within a hundred years after they were painted, it was almost impossible for a collector to obtain one. That is, the quality of these pictures, the fact that the world's great museums own a large share of them, has placed a premium price on the few now available to collectors. Renoir's work, described above in such shocking terms, now brings up to two hundred thousand dollars a picture, to name but one of the painters damned by the critical fraternity. It is not enough that we ignore these men, or consider them amusing or mad. We must, as a French humorist suggested, see that these dead men are really killed.

The critics of George Gershwin were never so ugly, ignorant, or misinformed. But many discerning people believe the lack of acceptance of his serious work was inexcusable. Although Satie and Debussy had made efforts to employ American popular styles, neither Stravinsky's *ragtime* nor Milhaud's *La Création du Monde,* nor Gershwin's *Rhapsody in Blue* seemed to have had any effect on current musical thought. The intelligentsia smilingly regarded these efforts as *hors-d'oeuvres;* spicy, trivial, evanescent. This is much more understandable, if one is to forgive at all, than what happened with the advent of *Porgy and Bess.* In retrospect, one reads the reviews with dismay and sadness. How could men have denied themselves so much pleasure, musical excitement, and deep emotional experience? Olin Downes, taking his prejudice with him to the theater, found "it does not utilize all the resources of the operatic composer, or pierce very often to the depths of the pathetic drama. The style is one moment of opera, and another of operetta or sheer Broadway entertainment."

Samuel Chotzinoff, himself an excellent musician, could see no further than that *Porgy and Bess* "as entertainment is hybrid, fluctuating constantly between music-drama, musical comedy, and operetta." But the most surprising of all the lukewarm or hostile criticisms came from Lawrence Gilman, a sensitive man of wide learning. Ordinarily his mind was very receptive. He said:

Perhaps it is needlessly Draconian to begrudge Mr. Gershwin the song hits which he has scattered through the score and which will doubtless enhance his fame and popularity. Yet they mar it. They are cardinal weaknesses. They are the blemish upon its musical integrity. Listening to such sure-fire rubbish as the duet between Porgy and Bess, "You is my woman now" ... you wonder how the composer could stoop to such easy and such needless conquests.

What were the climate and environment that produced a group of critics unable to meet and come to terms with a great new musical form and expression? These men shared a common cultural background. All of them had experienced that remarkable release of forces in all categories which occurred around the turn of the century. Freud, Jung, and Adler had made us aware of the discoveries of psychology and psychiatry. New developments had occurred in logic, chemistry, neurology, biology, aerodynamics, mathematics, and physics. All these new concepts were given an accelerated pace by dynamic changes in transportation and communication. Materials and products, formerly the result of laborious handwork, began to emerge in speedily fabricated quantities from machines. The release seemed to affect everything.

Virile artists, sickened by the banal and sentimental state of painting, insisted upon a new beginning. Cézanne, an unrecognized giant, had begun the process of returning painting to its logical and vital purposes through the intelligent employment of color, form, and construction. Others, including the unprecedented Picasso, had returned to such simple shapes as the cube, the cone, and the cylinder, and *cubism*, a powerful new influence, was born. Kandinsky, the first truly non-representational artist, and a few others of lesser stature, had brought to the fore a new sense and employment of space relationships. Painters were on the way with fellow insurgents in every field of life. Floundering in the word-ridden Victorian swamps of formless romanticism, literature suddenly ceased to be a meaningless imitation of past glories, and responded to the galvanizing ministrations of James Joyce, e. e. cummings, Gertrude Stein, and a host of younger writers, including the powerful Hemingway. Flying became practical and there were sensational exploits. Radio and the record took music to the millions. Newspapers and magazines and books came off the press in millions of copies, and a new spirit infused the theater, while the movies made rapid strides.

But musical growth and expansion in America took the form of more and more opportunity to hear music of the *past*, largely a *European* music. The Metropolitan Opera House, administered by the outwardly dignified Gatti-Casazza, offered a repertoire exclusively *Italian* and *German*. Hammerstein came with his Manhattan Opera House, a *French* company. The battle which ensued with the Metropolitan kept the American public diverted and amused. Mary Garden dazzled audiences with her interpretations of Mélisande, Thaïs, Carmen, Salomé, and other new, colorful roles. We possessed more large symphony orchestras than all Europe. America, so everyone said, was the most musical country in the world. But was it? American artists, without European credentials, languished in limbo.

A Scriabine, or a Ravel, or a Respighi would be brought over for a tour of the States. Our critics greeted them as caviar, interesting, yes, but of small importance in the world of the *great* composers. We were mostly preoccupied with the concert tours of the spectacular operatic and concert stars. New York recitals which took place at Carnegie Hall, Aeolian Hall, and later Town Hall, were the regular routine assignments of the critics, along with performances of the Metropolitan Opera, Hammerstein novelties, and, later, visits of the Chicago Opera Company. This was the standard musical fare. Wagner, Verdi, Puccini were the stand-bys at the Metropolitan. The programs of the symphony orchestras, the New York Symphony under Walter Damrosch, the New York Philharmonic with Josef Stransky, and later the New York Philharmonic Symphony with guest conductors, stuck close to Brahms, Beethoven, and Bach.

Then came the kaleidoscopic Diaghileff Ballet, under the banner of Otto Kahn and the Board of the Metropolitan Opera Company, America heard for the first time the music of Stravinsky, which shook everyone. But the critics were able to delay the day of reckoning with Stravinsky; they could pass him off as a *ballet* composer. That Stravinsky's music is even more balanced, unified, and glowing in color and form as *pure* or symphonic music never reached them. They faced the old, not the new, Europe. Unaware of what American jazz had done to revitalize popular music, they appeared unaware of the new world of painting, literature, or music.

Then Gershwin arrived.

Everything was against him. He was Tin Pan Alley. He was

successful. He was an American. He was facile. And, worst of all, he took a lot of liberties.

The critics did not like liberties of any kind. Witness the day the newly appointed impresario from La Scala arrived in New York to take charge of the Metropolitan Opera. Reporters boarded the ship at Ambrose Light. As they interviewed the imperturbable Gatti-Casazza in his stateroom, a handsome woman interrupted the interview. "Who is that?" the reporters demanded. "This is Madame Frances Alda, my mistress," the continental manager answered. There was a tremendous storm when the story broke. The critics met with the board members of the Metropolitan—whose wives had already met with *them*—and the high moral standards of the critics somehow coincided with the high moral standards of the august board. Later that day the bewildered Gatti-Casazza was informed, "In America we do not have mistresses." Some say Alda had been angling for Gatti to make it permanent for several years, that she took this method of making sure. If so, she knew her America, for in less than a week they were married.

The *Rhapsody* was jazz, and everybody loved Paul Whiteman. The *American in Paris* had been conducted by Walter Damrosch, than whom there was no more respectable and respected man. The *Concerto* was all right, colorful, rhythmic, but a distinctly minor work.

But *Porgy and Bess*. Who ever heard of an opera with Negroes? Who ever heard of a libretto in which a girl is raped, unless, of course, she is wronged in French, German, or Italian? Who ever heard of jazz aspiring to be opera? And who ever heard of an opera that could really move an audience to tears, where there were no diamond chokers and Hattie Carnegie gowns for the tears to fall on? Gershwin was all to _Merle_,

     With greatest en-
thusiasm for him as man,
and super - impresario.
And best wishes,

       George Gershwin

Mar. 4, 1937.

Self-portrait and inscription by G. G.

right for a now-and-then number on a symphony program. Or for recordings. Or for the young people dancing at night clubs. But now this brassy, vital young man had gone too far. He should know his place. Back to Broadway!

And this, simplified to be sure, was the atmosphere, the attitude, with which George Gershwin and his *Porgy and Bess* were faced. It is remarkable that it survived. However, the Gershwin name brought people to the theater, and the people, ignorant for the most part of opera, loved it. That was just the beginning.

Almost no one, with the exception of George and Ira and a few of their friends, felt there was any great future for this strange, moving, powerful opus; a work without category. The lack of category in which to put *Porgy and Bess* had been one of its chief handicaps. We will see how the tide began to turn, as we consider Olin Downes.

Downes was a large, robust-looking man with a friendly smile. He had a host of friends, and hundreds courted him for what he might be able to do for them in the columns of the powerful *Times*. When he came into my consciousness at Boston he was extremely friendly, as compared with the awesome Philip Hale, the austere H. T. Parker, Boston's contribution to the international fraternity of critics.

I saw Downes regularly over the years; we were associated indirectly and directly in several ventures, including the launching of a prodigy conductor, Loren Mazzel. When I removed my operations to California, Downes was my guest one summer while he was doing a series of articles on the Hollywood Bowl. We spent two days in Santa Barbara, with Henry Eichheim, for a discussion of oriental music. During my tour of the Philadelphia Orchestra with Leopold Stokowski, he was very much in the picture; he was astounded when in Los Angeles we broke world attendance records for a symphony orchestra presented indoors.

It was over modern music that we had our bitterest feuds, our most surprising encounters. When I was using Kandinsky to illustrate some of the forms of contemporary composers, he stopped me by asking who Kandinsky was. I took him to an exhibition of the work of Kandinsky at the Guggenheim Museum the following week, and Downes was bewildered. "How long has this sort of thing been going on?" he asked. A hurried and very brief explanation of what had really been going on in painting meant nothing to him. "It's just a fad," was his answer.

On the subject of Stravinsky he could be very ugly indeed. In his eyes Stravinsky had practically *no* merit. The earlier works he could hear as novelties. "Colorful and with a rude vitality," he would admit. But his special disdain was reserved for the later works, "Just empty cerebration for musical snobs." His man was Sibelius. When I suggested that Sibelius was in no sense a modern composer, that Sibelius was under the influence of Berlioz, Wagner, and Debussy, Downes pronounced me an idiot.

My last contact with Downes, about a year before he died, was over a book on which we collaborated as writer and designer. Its title explains it, *Ten Operatic Masterpieces.* Leonard Marker, a fine pianist and pupil of Schoenberg, made piano transcriptions of the ten operas. Downes rewrote his stories of the operas *six different times* in manuscript. We were impressed with his complete lack of decision about *anything.* This led to his rewriting each story at least seven times after it was in galley and page proofs, an exasperating, delaying, and expensive procedure. He had seen and heard these operas all his life; his was indeed a curious performance.

The agony of his ordeal impressed me, and I gave him special attention every time he visited my apartment. His uncertainty and lack of a frame of reference about the most important mutations of our time seemed to me pitiable, and I grew to have a certain compassion for him. But this was rudely erased. In November 1957, while I was making preparations for this book, a friend sent me a clipping from the New York *Times* of July 18, 1937, written by Olin Downes. It was an editorial written after George's death and it did not even mention *Porgy and Bess!*

Naturally the music of Gershwin was a challenge to the personal feelings the critics had about George Gershwin, the Broadway success, and often his assurance which was mistaken for immodesty by them. George moved among a group of people essentially of the theater. Writers, actors, singers, and others created an aura which, in the eyes of the more conventional and studious men, was flamboyant. How could a man who made a fortune with jazz be a serious musician?

After observing the critics in action I began to speculate on the precise role of the critic. What is the role of the critic and what are his accomplishments and his contributions to the arts? What changes have come to his role with the passing of time? I found that a number of men had been impressed with the same ideas, and had asked and found answers to some of the same questions.

Criticism in the modern sense, the advocacy and defense of new developments in music, painting, sculpture, literature, and poetry, began well before World War I. It stood on two pedestals. On one basis, it was an attempt to find the relationship of the living present with the traditions of the living past; on the other, it was an attack against the last wave of the Romantic movement with its stultifying and effete attitude toward all the arts. As Stephen Spender has stated it:

The letters of Ezra Pound, the early essays of T. S. Eliot, the polemics of Wyndham Lewis . . . were aspects of this aggressively and defensively creative movement. All these artists turned critics were extremely dubious of any criticism not written by critics who were themselves practicing artists. Thus Wyndham Lewis wrote that no one who was not himself a sculptor or painter could say anything of the slightest value about sculpture or painting. And Eliot in *The Function of Criticism* expressed his idea of the critical activity as "a kind of union with creation in the labor of the artist," and his misgivings before the work of critics who did not practice, and practice well, the arts they criticized.

Today, the wheel appears to have come full circle; there have grown new schools of academic critics equipped with the intellectual weapons of the self-defending poets of a previous generation, and devoting themselves to the "examination" through analysis, exegesis, and highly intellectualized standards, of every contemporary work that strikes their attention.

No one would deny the right, or the province of the critic. His role as encourager, explainer, and protector of the creative artist has been increasingly productive. But the important mistakes and misunderstandings are staggering. This is without question due to a fundamental element, the line which divides "the proper territory of original creation from the proper territory of criticism."

The contemporary critics of George Gershwin crossed this line time after time. They presented theories, musical traditions, and rules and matters of techniques, to prove that Gershwin was not, and could not be, a serious composer. If they had simply been tedious and difficult, small damage would have been done. But, instead, they were in such positions of power, and their authority so firmly established, that it made it virtually impossible for "men with new things to say, and new forms in which to express these things, to emerge."

The critic lives in a special world. He hears, senses, analyzes, researches, and goes to the past for his guides to the future. He often ignores the fact that any significant new work must have a quality of strangeness; otherwise no new statement has been made. And he most certainly fails in his duty if he does not make allowance for the fact "that in the contemporary work there will be some completely new element which comes out of contemporary life and which he cannot at all judge. . . . The critic is exceptionally aware of precedent. The original artist is terrifyingly familiar with the unprecedented."

It has taken the loyal enthusiasm of a discriminating worldwide public, a group of courageous entrepreneurs, and a whole new generation of critics to disclose the importance of George Gershwin's contribution, and to reveal its significance.

One can now say without fear of successful contradiction that George Gershwin is our greatest composer to date, and one of the few men in the contemporary world's music who have *invented* new forms, and *discovered* new modes.

From 135th Street, the one-act opera written in 1922, to *Porgy and Bess* in 1935, is but thirteen years. Besides his theater music and songs, Gershwin wrote his major works in this short, crowded period.

A great many of the critics have held that the music of George Gershwin is *vulgar*, that he is a *vulgar* composer. Twelve people will hold twelve different views. Webster defines *vulgar*: "Of or belonging to, or common to the great mass of people. Characterized by a lack of culture, refinement, taste, sensitivity, etc.; coarse, crude, boorish." In this category it is impossible to put the music of Gershwin. But if we accept another category of "vulgarity," often applied to such composers as Chabrier, Bizet, Albéniz, Glinka, Rimsky-Korsakoff, Tchaikovsky, Schubert, many passages in Wagner, and some of the works of Milhaud, Satie, and Auric, we are far nearer the mark. This kind of vulgarity is broad enough to contain musical motives popular in origin and character, organizing the sentimental, buoyantly erotic, salty, charming, and earthy values common to us all. Much of the music of Smetana, Dvořák, and Stephen Foster is vulgar use of vulgar material. The line where vulgarity slips into banality, below the level of acceptance, is personified by the music of the Russian contemporary, Khachaturian. The manner in which vulgar material is used separates the tawdry from the intelligent and vital.

Paul Rosenfeld, a critic powerful with the intellectuals, and one of the most sensitive tasters and writers who was active in the time of Gershwin, thought that George's music was even below the vulgar level. Many of Rosenfeld's judgments were distinguished, discerning, and just. He was a champion of many creators who have left their mark, Georgia O'Keeffe, Alfred Stieglitz, John Marin, Arthur Dove, Marsden Hartley, Edgar Varèse, Aaron Copland, e. e. cummings, and others. Also he had a stubbornness and a myopia almost unforgivable. He would never read Mark Twain because someone had told him Twain was coarse and brash. Friends gave him *Tom Sawyer, Huckleberry Finn,* and *Innocents Abroad* to read. He never opened them. But he could elect to present Leo Ornstein as a great new note in music. This lays him open to grave suspicion as a prophet. It is all the more remarkable when his background is understood. Paul Rosenfeld sought the new in all phases of American art. He believed that great aesthetic works would emerge in this country, and he consciously looked for them. He certainly found many and was of a singular comfort and support to those he elected to champion. His monument is secure in this undisputed service.

But a man who will champion Leo Ornstein and reject George Gershwin is limited or prejudiced, or both. He says:

True, at moments in the *Piano Concerto* and *An American in Paris*, an idea, curiously enough a tragic one, of an inevitable chaos, a predestinately incomplete and unsuccessful connection between complementary forces, feebly glimmers on one. But its glimmer is fickle and disappears as the form itself loses its impulse and falls into idle repetitions and meaningless flourishes. The whole, if it points to anything, points to a creative energy too feeble and unenduring to afford sustained contact with reality and a mind that, lacking creative power, remains the prisoner of by no means idealistic dreams. It is impossible to hear Gershwin's symphonic music without being from time to time moved by its grandiloquences to conceive—with the aspect of things having some immensely flattering, glorifying bearing upon ourselves—of towers of fine gold rising amid Florida palms, splendiferous hotel foyers crowded with important people and gorgeous women *décolletées jusque là*, and immediately contingent upon paradise; or rosy bank of nymphs amorously swooning amid bells of rose-pink tulle. A tawny oriental city acknowledges us as its conqueror in the sundown, and the superb naked woman who stands above the city gate, starred with the diamond in her tresses, descends and advances toward us with exalted words and gestures, hailing our peerlessness while we ourselves recognize in her the one we have always sought and loved. Are these atrocious dreams our own? Possibly, but they have grown articulate through this music.

Of *Porgy and Bess,* Paul Rosenfeld pontificates:

> The score is a loose aggregation of somewhat heavily instrumentated numbers in many instances conforming to the style of American Negro music, especially the blues, and in others to that of Puccini grand opera. Some of the pieces, for example the entire thunderstorm music, are very bad and empty; others—one thinks particularly of the lullaby and the fugue in Scene I, the antiphonies of chorus and solos in the scene of the wake, and certain popular numbers—have a quality and sensuous charm and flavor. An aggrandized musical show ... but the score sustains no mood. There is neither a progressive nor an enduring tension in it. Nor do they communicate reality, either the rich, authentic quality of the Negro or the experience of Porgy, the pathetic cripple.... It would seem as if Gershwin knew chiefly stage Negroes and that he very incompletely felt the drama of the two protagonists. ... Long before the conclusion one feels the music has got one nowhere new and true.

This incredible estimate comes perilously close to Bernard Berenson's uncomprehending fulminations against Matisse, Picasso, and other powerful contemporary painters. It is embarrassing and unfortunately conclusive.

Alfred Frankenstein has written a very perspicacious and clear statement about the mind and attitude of Rosenfeld, some parts of which I here quote:

> Rosenfeld observes in *An Hour with American Music* that the nature of a piece of music depends upon the "state" of the composer at the time of composition. The phrase, to be sure, is not amplified, but in its context it seems to imply that the whole art of music is merely a series of accidents produced by external circumstances which have thrown musically sensitive people into creative "states": that music has its own independent life and validity is only feebly apprehended. The end of the nineteenth

century was indeed a pathetic era in music. After the *Sacre,* an ethic era was born, and Rosenfeld was present at its *accouchement.* At first he was utterly bewildered by it. He called it "cerebral formalism," "archaicizing," or "diddling with fugues." Later he condemned it as a sign of postwar confusion and weakness, a passing fad, and predicted it would soon pass. But in 1927 he blamed it on a lamentable externalism which is characteristic of the French mind and on Eric Satie as its immediate source. The next year, Camille Saint-Saëns is the villain of the piece; later yet, when he had begun to make his peace with it, he traced it to Busoni. Ultimately, however, he did see that his new orientation in music was a thing of immense importance and one very characteristic of our own time. He can scarcely be criticized for not having seen it sooner, partly because it came, like many manifestations in art, in the form of a pendulum swing that went far back, at least in some externals, and so seemed to be a dislocation.

This seems eminently fair to Paul Rosenfeld and at the same time reveals an instability of judgment and a surprising lack of profundity in his knowledge and evaluations. The swing of the pendulum of which Frankenstein speaks has always interested me, and seems a recurrent phenomenon. In 1944, when I was completing *Accent on America,* my autobiography, as an antidote to Air Force life and problems, I played with this idea as follows:

To my eyes and ears, there is far more relationship between the great contemporary creators and the men of the thirteenth to sixteenth centuries, than exists between the moderns and the masters of the Romantic or middle period. Would not Giotto, Fra Angelico, Uccello, Francesca, Botticelli, Bellini, Mantegna, Fouquet, Brueghel, and El Greco have understood the best contemporary painters, including the abstractionists, much better than they would have the Gainsboroughs, Corots, Constables,

Fragonards, and other Romantics, including Rembrandt and Velázquez? Are we witnessing the conclusion of a cycle? The return again to the so-called primitive interest in form has a sound aesthetic basis.

One may ask the same about Pergolesi, Palestrina, Mozart, and Bach. My judgment is that their sympathy would be with the great contemporary composers, as against the music of Schumann, Schubert, Liszt, Wagner, and particularly the works of Verdi and Puccini. Again the pendulum swings.

Rosenfeld was prejudiced by Gershwin's Broadway success, and he loathed jazz. Critics and people generally who find jazz bestial, undisciplined, and crass were naturally unable to accept the Gershwin fare. If one dislikes sour cream, then the delicacies of sour-cream dishes, bitki, stroganoff, borsch, and many other succulent and savory experiences, are closed to him.

But the real difficulty is that which has greeted every creator, inventor, and scientist of substance. One can pursue this theme into a metaphysical realm of diminishing returns and become lost in sterile speculation. But obviously there comes an arrestation, a terminus, a point beyond which many honest persons cannot go with conviction. The Air Force speaks of a plane's ceiling. Every human being has a ceiling.

These ceilings have provided me with some rare experiences. Well do I recall a performance of the Philharmonic at Carnegie Hall, when both the orchestra players and the audience alike laughed outright at parts of *Petrouchka*. Paul Althouse in years past gave a concert version of *Boris Godunoff* in New York assisted by Matzenaurer and stars of the Metropolitan; more audience laughter. When Edgar Varèse's *Ionisation* was performed in the Hollywood Bowl a dozen years ago, friends, who were ardent supporters of the Bowl, leaned over and whispered to my box party that, if ever such a disgraceful thing happened again in the Bowl, they would withdraw their support. They spent the balance of the playing time for this vigorous composition in hissing.

The inability to make the transition to Gershwin on the part of critics was not of the same sort or degree as the audience reactions cited above. It was both a more informed and a more conditioned estrangement. Their outlook, attitude, and training looked in another direction. Music was the music of Europe; there was no other music worthy of serious attention.

So strong was this European *influence* that few sensitive Americans could respond to anything but the most self-consciously aesthetic aspects of diluted culture. Subject them to the terrifyingly magnificent tribal dances of the Hopi or Navajo, to the humor of Ring Lardner, to the comparatively simple and graceful architecture of Louis Sullivan, or other evidences of native or invented American vitality, and the result was either bafflement or annoyance.

The gaudy, cheap, and obscene images which the music of Gershwin created for Paul Rosenfeld were perfectly honest for him. He was a removed observer, an aesthetic dandy. The uproarious things which were daily happening all over America as it sprang toward its "manifest destiny" were unknown to him, and had they been known, would have been distasteful.

He wanted new art and music to be born in America, but on his terms. He wanted them to be a continuation of what his own mind and response told him was important. When it came in the sense of the music of Gershwin he was repelled, and his only response was insulting ridicule. Had he experienced a bit of the cowboy life of Texas; spent some time with the oil workers of Oklahoma; breathed the same air as the Gullah negroes in the Carolinas; or ridden a mile-long "fruit block" crossing the continent back of a majestic Mallet . . . if you can possibly imagine the incongruity of Paul Rosenfeld in such situations, you have the answer.

In Paul's world, these things did not exist. But it is from this America, the workaday and mechanized America, that Gershwin stems. And it is this pungency, this closeness to *the soil, the action, the people's vitality* that gave Gershwin's work its passport, that supplies its identity and validity.

Few people today can understand what a power Paul Rosenfeld once exerted in the aesthetic world. He wrote regularly for *The Dial*, an extraordinary publication with unrivaled influence in the world of art, literature, and music. Rosenfeld wrote for other journals and one leading New York newspaper. It was because he was so highly respected and so generally right in his judgments and discernment that his misunderstanding of George Gershwin was so important, and so discouraging. We are all entitled to miss the target not once, but many times. The spirit of this discussion is not that of an attack on this eminent man. His own words, supposedly considered judgments, convict him. They are printed words, and thereby doubly powerful.

To give the true picture of what confronted Gershwin, it was necessary to bring Paul Rosenfeld into this book as a major factor. Paul Rosenfeld was one of George's great stumbling blocks, one of the influences that clouded his skies. Other generations, who may look upon this book or indeed this generation, will have a clearer picture of the currents, the controversies, and the generally uncertain attitudes that prevailed while George Gershwin proceeded on his way toward his own goals and with his own convictions.

Nothing dies as hard as an attitude. Once an attitude has been expressed by learned and respected men and has gone into books of history, criticism, psychology, and even fiction it becomes a stubborn, almost indestructible force. The American attitude has become a constructive force that encourages millions, gives motivation to progress, and binds us together. But as time outmodes certain of its tenets, these are not necessarily eliminated from our books, our teaching, or our consciousness.

For instance, too large a number of Americans still look back to Europe as our spiritual, intellectual, and psychological home. Changes have come so fast in our country that Americans are unaware of the gulf that separates our attitudes and our thinking. From the very beginning, from the time of the forming of the thirteen original colonies, we have possessed an inferiority complex about Europe. I mention it here because it was the basic underlying cause of the rejection of Gershwin, particularly of his *Porgy and Bess*.

Just how old and how deep is this attitude is beautifully demonstrated by an article written by a remarkable man who was born in Boston in 1805. He was one of the first to be articulate in championing the American spirit. His name was Horatio Greenough. Educated at Harvard, he spent most of his early life in Florence where as a sculptor he produced many portrait busts, single figures, and bas-reliefs for Italy. Back in America his many distinguished sitters included John Quincy Adams, Lafayette, and James Fenimore Cooper. His perceptive ideas about Europe and America read like a progressive contemporary. Says he, at about the year 1850:

The susceptibility, the tastes and the genius which enable a people to enjoy the fine arts and to excel in them have been denied to the Anglo-Americans not only by European talkers, but by European thinkers. The assertion of our obtuseness and inefficiency in this respect has been ignorantly and presumptuously set forth by some persons merely to fill up the measure of our condemnation. Others have arrived at the same conclusion after examining our political and social character, after investigating our exploits, and testing our capacities. They admit that we trade with enterprise and skill, that we build ships cunningly and sail them well, that we have a quick and farsighted apprehension of the value of a territory, that we make wholesome homespun laws for its government, and that we fight hard when molested in any of these homely exercises in our ability; but they assert that there is a stubborn, antipoetical tendency in all that we do or say or think; they attribute our very excellence in the ordinary business of life to causes which must prevent our development as artists. Enjoying the accumulated result of the thought and labor of centuries, Europe has witnessed our struggles with the hardships of an untamed continent and the disadvantages of colonial relations with only a partial appreciation of what we aim at; with but an imperfect knowledge of what we have done. Seeing us intently occupied during several generations in felling forests, building towns, and constructing roads, she thence formed a theory that we are good for nothing except these pioneer efforts. She taunted us because there were no statues or frescoes in our log cabins; she pronounced us unmusical because we did not sit down in the swamp, with an Indian on one side and a rattlesnake on the other, to play the violin. That she should triumph over the deficiencies of a people who had set the example of revolt and republicanism was natural; but the reason she assigned for these deficiencies was not the true reason. She argued with the depth and the sagacity of a philosopher who could conclude from seeing an infant imbibe with eagerness its first aliment that its whole life would be occupied in similar absorption.

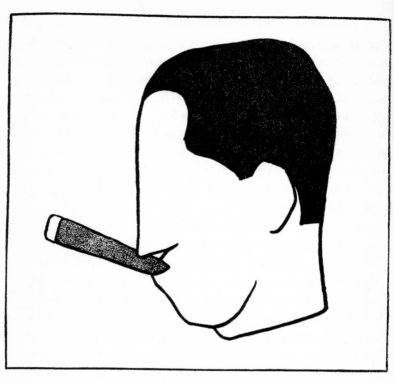

G. G. by Auerbach-Levy

Possibly few men possess the enlightenment and discernment of a Greenough, whose gently sarcastic comments might have been written yesterday. Nor is critical discernment confined to any one period, any one intellectual plane or profession. Although many critics missed the point of Gershwin's exciting music, there were many perspicacious composers and performers who had a very different reaction. This book gives me an opportunity to review the attitudes of some of Gershwin's most distinguished contemporaries.

The composer Stravinsky has some very sound ideas about his contemporaries, and there are performers who possess the keenest insight in evaluating creators. My contact with Stravinsky's music goes back to 1916 when the Serge de Diaghileff Ballet burst upon America. Since then Stravinsky has become a great friend of mine. I have visited him in Paris and he has been my guest in America. I have produced two books on this great composer. When he and Samuel Dushkin, the violinist, were playing concerts under my management, they both came to dinner and to spend an evening. Stravinsky, a week before, had inquired about my record collection and particularly wanted to know what Gershwin recordings I possessed. I assured him that my albums contained everything available of a major nature that Gershwin had written. After their arrival and while cocktails were being served, Stravinsky started to go through the record racks, pulling out all the Gershwin records he could find. He began playing them before dinner, and again, as soon as dinner was finished, he went back to the record player. Seated about ten feet away from the loud-speaker, Stravinsky conducted as each of the Gershwin works was played. He completely lost himself for nearly three hours, sometimes repeating a record or portions of it many times. As they departed at midnight, Stravinsky said: "This is fascinating, this is America. This Gershwin is a *very* talented man."

Then there was the time when I was so immersed in the affairs of the great Russian bass that my friends called it my "Chaliapin period." In his unprecedented rise from a lowly Volga boatman to world eminence, Chaliapin had grown tremendously in wisdom and his observations were very keen. America fascinated him. All Americans seemed to him to have been born rich, educated, and successful. "If Americans can start from such a high platform, think of the great heights they will eventually reach. They have no inborn inferiority complexes, no lack of confidence in themselves or their future," he told me one afternoon as we consumed a magnum of champagne. "Take a man like your Gershwin. He was born for America, he feels America, he is America. The admiration I have for this country is tremendous; your advancement in every material way takes the breath away. But I never expected much in the way of art. Gershwin is beginning to convince me that art can come from a mechanized civilization, too. I wish I might live to see more Americans tackle art with the flair they have for everything else."

There may be some readers of this book who will remember when Charles L. Wagner and I brought Walter Gieseking to this country. We three had quite a controversy, a very gentle controversy, I must say, over what kind of program he should play at his debut. Beginning with Rachmaninoff and Hofmann, every pianist had been playing almost the same type of program in the preceding two concert seasons. All of us finally agreed on a radical departure. Gieseking would make his debut in the New World playing a program of half Bach, half Debussy. He did, and he made history. In the following seasons on tour, we had two favorite subjects of conversation. One was butterflies, for Gieseking was a devoted and enthusiastic lover of lepidoptera. The other was the future of music in America, and of Gershwin in particular.

Since I had never had a butterfly net in my hand, I am sure Gieseking found my butterfly conversation rather dull. About all I could tell him was that swarms of them once stopped Santa Fe trains in the Middle West; there were so many thousands of them resting on the rails, that locomotive wheels could not get traction to pull the trains. But on the subject of music and Gershwin we fused. Gieseking had some curious ideas. He believed that someday the United States would be a musical giant because we were not a warlike people. "War creates armies, and armies create generals, and the public creates gods from generals. Did you know that even so great a man as Spengler was a cringing, supine figure in the presence of generals? Generals did not like the *music* of Wagner except for their pride that he was German, they like it because it dealt with the mythology of the gods! War and music are impossible."

As for Gershwin, Gieseking thought he was the result of forces, multiple forces, converging at the right moment. "George Gershwin had a Jewish father and mother who must have come together at the precise and proper moment. George had an interest in and a sympathy for the Negro and his problems. George was born at the precise moment when America was on the move, when everything was burgeoning with energy and creation. So the forces of the Jew, the Negro, the new land of creation, flowered in a few men, and one of the rare ones was Gershwin." I asked him if this was not indeed a mystical concept, and he replied, "What isn't?"

Then he told me that he was not temperamentally equipped to play Gershwin in public, but that in Europe he frequently played George's music for his friends. When he had a few idle hours before a concert in various cities around the country on tour, Gieseking and I would go to music shops and play the new Gershwin records, either popular or serious. "He's got it in both his popular and his serious works," Gieseking maintained.

Among the amenities of managing tenors and coloraturas, not to mention operatic legends such as Mary Garden, are the opportunities for hearing the off-beat experiences and secret ambitions which are confided to you on long train journeys.

Mary Garden had been a close friend of Debussy, and in addition to having created the role of Mélisande, she had worked a great deal with the great French master on such works as *La Demoiselle Élue* and *The Songs of Bilitis*.

Mary Garden had become interested in the things Gershwin was doing for the theater, and it was my pleasure to introduce her to the *Concerto in F* and the *Rhapsody in Blue*. She was astounded. She was a very contemporary-minded woman, with a daring which had made her famous, and to her Gershwin really meant an important forward step in music. But knowing the grueling hours, days, and months she had devoted to just one operatic role, she was flabbergasted that Gershwin could produce the fresh style and invention of his serious work and at the same time turn out such amazing theatrical concoctions, as she called them. "How does he do it?" she asked over and over again whenever Gershwin came into our conversation.

I managed the final concert tour which Mary Garden made in America, a recital devoted entirely to the arias and songs of Debussy, with a thirty-minute interlude in which she told her enchanted audiences about the personal life and times of the great composer. On this tour she confided that she was going to open a school in Paris "in not too many years," and that she thought Gershwin should be on her faculty. "And, Armitage, you have got to get him for me," she said, when I saw her off for Europe in the spring.

Gershwin had another admirer in John McCormack. Despite his enormous popular success—he holds many box-office records for the world—John was also a "musicians' musician." His Mozart was flawless in style and he was constantly besieged by the conductors of our great symphony orchestras with requests to appear as soloist. With the enormous guarantee

which we were paying McCormack, we could accept but few
of these engagements, as fees for soli appearances with orchestra amounted to about one third what we could gross in
concerts. John McCormack had been a failure when Hammerstein had brought him to America to appear with his
Manhattan Opera Company. Remembering this, John was
fascinated with the dilemma of Gershwin. "How Gershwin
can rise above his spectacular success as a writer of shows
and popular songs I cannot see," said McCormack to me.
"But Gershwin is so courageous that he haunts me."

McCormack and Fritz Kreisler were close friends, on a
musical as well as a social basis. One night at a dinner which
Kreisler gave McCormack both artists had invited their managers. Charles Ellis of Boston handled Kreisler's affairs, while
McCormack had entrusted his career to Charles L. Wagner
and myself. During the evening the subject, thanks to the
managers, got off strictly aesthetic-musical ground and onto
careers in America and the financial rewards of those who were
successful. It developed into a really sparkling examination of
the Gershwin position. As another friend Erle Stanley Gardner
would have put it, it became "The Case of the Popular
Genius." Charles Ellis, a very astute man who had been responsible to a great degree for the American fortunes of
Kreisler, Farrar, Paderewski, and others, thought Gershwin's
was simply a flash-in-the-pan success which would soon sub-
side. "His tantalizing rhythms which get him where he is are
as evanescent as fog, and will as soon disappear," was his
dictum. Kreisler was not at all sure that he would disappear so
easily. "I have written some songs, as you know, and even an
operetta," he observed, "and you can take my word for it
that the facility of Gershwin is deceptive. He has introduced
something that may very well be the voice of America." It is

a privilege for me to present this testimony of a most perspicacious musician, and I believe for the first time in print.

Galli-Curci seemed the least likely even to know that Gershwin existed. This Italian coloratura had been the greatest gamble that Wagner and I had ever taken, for she was completely unknown when we sent her out on an American tour to replace the opulent-voiced Emmy Destinn, after this creator of the role of *Girl of the Golden West* had been forbidden to leave Germany by the Kaiser for her criticism of him during World War I. Among the dozens of cities that afterward clamored for a Galli-Curci concert was South Bend, Indiana. I dropped off a New York Central train one morning to look over the prospects, and could find but one theater which seated only 1,200 persons, whereas we needed a house that seated at least 3,000 people for a Galli-Curci event.

As it was several hours before another train could take me on to Chicago, I taxied out to Notre Dame University to watch football practice. Knute Rockne was putting his first team through their paces. He knew me through our mutual friend John McCormack. He spied me in the bleachers, stopped the practice, and came over for a chat. He asked what on earth I was doing on the university campus, and I told him of my frustration about a Galli-Curci concert in South Bend. "Say, wait a minute," Rockne said. "I believe we may have a solution." He then told me that the huge old gymnasium, which had been outmoded by a new building, was at my disposal, if it would serve my purpose. "We don't have any chairs, but you can probably get them from the undertakers," Rockne added. After inspecting the great building, we went over to the administration building to get a confirmation of the deal from the university's president, after which I called the Coit-Alber Lyceum and Chautauqua people in Cleveland.

These people book lecturers all over America in summer, and play them in tents, using portable chairs. They were delighted to rent me 3,000 chairs, and we immediately made plans for a Galli-Curci concert in South Bend that season.

But when, on the fateful day that Galli-Curci arrived for the event, we took her out to look at an old building, with a dirt floor, a stage constructed of crude lumber and decorated with flower boxes "borrowed" from various South Bend homes, we knew we faced a problem. Galli-Curci was not amused. We went back to the hotel. On the way neither she, her husband-accompanist Homer Samuels, nor I said a word. But in the ensuing conference in Galli-Curci's suite, there were many words, many of them rather unkind.

Then the conversation took an unexpected turn. "If I go through with this rather undignified appearance, are you prepared to do something for me?" she queried. "Almost anything within reason," I replied, and told her every one of those 3,000 seats was sold and that we were selling standing room. "All right," she snapped. "We will cancel Madison, which is our next date, and I am going to leave right after tonight's concert for New York and the première of the new George Gershwin show."

Upsetting as this was to me, I realized that canceling Madison, with its auditorium seating but 1,800, and a management which had not been enthusiastic about Galli-Curci in the first place, was preferable to disappointing the South Bend audience, many of whom were coming fifty or more miles to hear her. The thing that finally persuaded me to accept this compromise was a telephone call from Chicago, which came at the precise moment, telling me that an entire Pullman full of notables was coming over to see if Galli-Curci was as enchanting in concert as Chicago knew her to be in opera. We made the deal ... and Galli made the Gershwin première, and at the end of the season, Galli-Curci sang one extra concert for us in Atlantic City just to prove, as she said, "that Gershwin was worth it" and that there were no hard feelings about South Bend, where she had received an ovation.

These are things that Gershwin never knew.

As George gained stature he simultaneously broadened his horizon. Although he still blushed when celebrities or composers such as Stravinsky, Ravel, Milhaud complimented him, he steadily consolidated his gains, to use a Wall Street term. He did not underestimate himself, but, more important, he did not overestimate himself either.

At the time that *Oh, Kay!* with Victor Moore was on Broadway, *Pro Musica*, a musical organization with chapters in many of the larger cities, brought Maurice Ravel to America for a tour. This was a considerable undertaking for them, and our office was able to do a number of chores which were beyond the scope of this small organization. This brought me into contact with Ravel on several occasions. His enthusiasm for Gershwin was genuine and he was most articulate about it. He saw *Oh, Kay!* three times, for instance, because of the Gershwin music. He was complimentary in a very handsome way about the *Concerto in F*.

In March of 1928 Eva Gauthier gave a party for Gershwin, and among other distinguished guests was Ravel, who had expressed a desire to meet Gershwin personally and hear him play. George obliged with an evening of music which the guests, particularly Ravel, found nothing short of stunning. Ravel talked so much about Gershwin that for a time I was almost convinced that he was overdoing it, in gratitude for our American hospitality. But the proof was soon forthcoming.

Ravel was commissioned to write a concerto for Paul Wittgenstein, the famed Austrian pianist who had lost an arm in World War I. As Ravel worked at the concerto, he was haunted by the jazz that had so fascinated him in the night clubs of New York, and more particularly by what Gershwin had done with the jazz idiom. Ravel decided to use many of the ideas which his American tour had inspired, and the result was the one-handed Wittgenstein concerto. The *Concerto for the Left Hand* is of course one of Ravel's most brilliant works, full of the peculiar tension which only jazz provides.

George began to meet other composers, including Milhaud, Poulenc, Auric, and Prokofieff. The latter was captivated by the rhythmic intricacies of Gershwin's music. He did not hesitate to say that George would make a great contribution to music if he could detach himself from, as he put it, "dollars and dinners."

It was an expansive period for George, and a difficult one. Broadway producers, on the one hand, kept up the pressure for more songs and shows. His serious associates, with great conviction, held out the promise of a permanent success on the highest plane. George kept his own counsel and made his own decision. And when late one evening he read the book of *Porgy* he was certain he had discovered a libretto for a someday opera.

5. George Gershwin, as the Legend Grew

GEORGE GERSHWIN: "I stood outside a penny arcade listening to an automatic piano leaping through Rubinstein's *Melody in F*; the peculiar jumps held me rooted."

One of his young friends possessed a piano, and George became a frequent visitor there; before long he tried to make up a piece of his own. The mere anticipation of spending time at the piano made blood rush to his face. As he worked out one melody and then another, he felt the excitement of exploration.

George met the young Max Rosenzweig, and they became boyhood pals. But Max, later the famous violinist Max Rosen, hurt George to the quick when he told him he would never be a musician. Later, George actually took over the piano that his mother had purchased with Ira in mind. Soon he was imploring his father for music lessons.

George played for the concert pianist and composer Charles Hambitzer, who took him as a pupil. Hambitzer was full of enthusiasm for his new pupil, pronouncing George a genius. He nevertheless regretted George's stubborn interest in "this modern stuff, jazz and what not."

Long after George was famous he wrote: "Irving Berlin was the first to free the American song from nauseating sentimentality; he gave us the first germ of an American musical idiom."

Another idol was Jerome Kern. George found him, like Irving Berlin, an exciting, compelling man to whom he listened breathlessly. He was even known to wait outside Kern's home, hoping to hear him play.

George discovered that Mozart, Beethoven, Schubert, and even Brahms had written popular music in their waltzes, country dances, and other idioms understood by the masses.

It was a great day when George finally met Irving Berlin at Remick's. Berlin patiently heard George play and tell of his ambitions. Berlin's consideration took the form of real encouragement. He assured George he would go far and advised him to "just keep plugging."

Turned down by publishers to whom he took his music, George kept on trying. Failure seemed to be an incentive for this young man.

Paul Whiteman to George Gershwin: "It is your music I want for my concert. Your music would be fresh and inspired. Theirs would only be manufactured."

DuBose Heyward on Gershwin: "A young man of enormous physical and emotional vitality, who possesses the faculty of seeing himself quite impersonally and realistically, and who knows exactly what he wants and where he is going. This characteristic puts him beyond modesty and conceit."

Reproved by his mother for taking over parties by playing his music, George told his mother firmly but gently that if he did not play, he just did not enjoy himself.

In Paris, George called on Maurice Ravel to see if he would take him as a pupil. Ravel assured him it was much better to be a first-class Gershwin than a second-class Ravel.

An apocryphal but witty story concerns Gershwin's asking to study with Stravinsky. Stravinsky countered by asking

Gershwin his yearly income. On being given a six-figure sum, Stravinsky said: "Why don't I study with you?"

From 135th Street (Blue Monday) in 1922 to Porgy and Bess in 1935 George seemed constantly obsessed with his desire to write an opera. In fact Blue Monday was already an attempt at writing a half-hour Negro opera; it not only impressed Paul Whiteman but foreshadowed Porgy and Bess. George once admitted to Jerome Kern that he had quite a bit of talent, and an enormous amount of nerve.

Isaac Goldberg speaks of George's Penthouse Idyll, "The lighting is indirect, there are Bellows lithographs, for George was a fight fan, and an excellent screen painted by Botkin, depicting in unashamed color various episodes in An American in Paris. It is Riverside Drive on the Hudson, George, just past thirty-three, moves easily, confidently, through the affluence and comfort he has won for himself. No affectations. Simplicity, and even at moments an engaging naïveté. The man and his music—and this, too, on his part is a form of honesty—are one."

Gershwin on himself: "When I am in my normal mood, the tunes come dripping off my fingers."

Goldberg: "He likes the notion of using chiefly tonic and dominant harmonies and getting his variety by writing, in the accented parts of the melody, notes that do not belong to the chord."

Of an Eva Gauthier recital at Aeolian Hall on Thursday evening, November 1, 1923, with songs by Berlin, Kern, and Gershwin, Deems Taylor said in the World: "The audience was as much fun to watch as the songs were to hear. It began by being just a trifle patronizing and ended by surrendering completely to the alluring rhythms of our own folk music."

George Gershwin on his brother Ira: "Never a worry. If not

today, tomorrow. That's how he always feels. Isn't it wonderful to feel that way?"

Ira Gershwin on George: "Nothing discourages him, always ready to jump into harness. Or tackle four things at a time. Isn't it wonderful to be that way?"

In 1926 came the jazz battle. Reverend John Roach Straton lashed out at the "music of the savage, intellectual and spiritual debauchery, utter degradation."

Were jazz adherents bandits and rattlesnakes? Was jazz bootleg music that should be outlawed? The exotic Peruvian singer, one of opera's best, Marguerite d'Alvarez said: "Nonsense. When I die, I want Gershwin's jazz concerto played over my grave."

Amy Lowell to George Gershwin in a conversation about jazz: "I can only move my toe to it, but if I couldn't do that, I think I should burst with the rapture of it."

The Preludes. Possibly the least-known Gershwin. Must be heard by anyone interested in the anatomy of George Gershwin's development. Should ballad and prelude moods and methods not be subjected to the jazz idiom?

Oscar Hammerstein II: "Maybe we took George too much for granted."

Carl Van Vechten, after the première of *Rhapsody in Blue*: "The concert, quite as a matter of course, was a riot; you crowned it with what I am forced to regard as the foremost serious effort by an American composer."

Paul Whiteman: "George thought always in orchestral terms, and he played in that fashion."

Rouben Mamoulian: "A man like George Gershwin never dies."

Todd Duncan: "A performance with George Gershwin as accompanist was a transcendent experience."

J. Rosamond Johnson: "George, you've done it—you're the Abraham Lincoln of Negro music."

Arnold Schoenberg: "An artist is like an apple tree. When his time comes, he bursts into bloom and starts to produce apples. And as an apple tree neither knows nor asks about the value experts of the market will attribute to his product, so a real composer does not ask whether his products will please the experts of serious art."

Serge Koussevitzky: "Like a rare flower which blossoms forth once in a great while, Gershwin represents a singularly original and rare phenomenon; the enchantment of this extraordinary being is too great to be real."

George Antheil: "George Gershwin mirrored us exactly. We need only to look into his music to see a whole period of our history."

Harold Arlen: "The humor, the satire, the playfulness of most of his melodic phrases were the natural expression of the man."

Leonard Liebling: "I witnessed George's triumphant appearance, playing the *Rhapsody* with the Minneapolis Symphony in its home town. Before that engagement Mr. McKnight, chairman of the board, wired me, 'Do you think this is the kind of music we ought to give our public?' I answered: 'It is the kind of music your public would resent not being given.'"

Otto H. Kahn: "In the rhythm, the melody, the humor, the grace, the rush and sweeps and dynamics of his compositions, he expresses the genius of young America."

Lester Donahue: "He was tremendously acquisitive about all phases of music and impressed me by delving into Bach at a time when he was still regarded only as a brilliant and promising composer of Broadway shows."

Ferde Grofé: "I will not meet the like of George Gershwin again, a rare and refined spirit, an innovator in American music and one who has left upon it a lasting imprint of new ideas voiced with bold originality."

Walter Damrosch: "I developed a strong affection for George personally and for the genuineness of his musical talent. To tell the truth, I tried to wean him from Broadway, as I felt he had it in him to develop on more serious lines."

Alexander Steinert: "George was a great perfectionist and whatever he undertook he did well, whether it was painting, photography, or sports. His love for modern painting was a dominant factor and the logical outcome of his aesthetic development."

Louis Danz: "In the history of music which has been composed in America the names of Arnold Schoenberg and George Gershwin may be linked together. In these two creative geniuses we have the fullest expression of today. Neither one nor the other could play from both sides of the net, but both play famously from the side of their choosing."

Irving Berlin:

> "I could speak of a Whiteman rehearsal
> At the old Palais Royal when Paul
> Played the *Rhapsody* that lifted Gershwin
> From the *Alley* to Carnegie Hall.
>
> I could dwell on the talent that placed him
> In the class where he justly belongs,
> But this verse is a song writer's tribute
> To a man who wrote wonderful songs."

Albert Heink Sendrey: "In order to create pure and poetic music and greater works of art, George needed praise and admiration as a flower needs sunshine and rain."

Jerome Kern: "There was never anything puny or insignificant about the life, work, or opinions of George Gershwin. He lived, labored, played, exulted, and suffered with bigness and gusto. It was some other contemporary, definitely *not* George, who was the subject of Thomas Mann's observation: 'Why does he make himself so little? Surely he is not that big.' "

Gilbert Seldes: "If George is going to do an opera this year, you may be sure that it fits into a general plan which may include a movie theme song, or a tone poem, or a popular melody for next year. If he decides not to compose for six months and amuse himself by painting, he will have in mind the results of his vacation on the next season's output. Gershwin is really Kipling's child with his 'satiable curiosity.' "

Henry Botkin: "During our many years of close relationship I have noted how the special quality of Gershwin's extraordinary music has given proof of the similarity of imaginative tendencies and strong spiritual kinship to many striking achievements in paint."

Isaac Goldberg: "Of technically skilled composers we had, and have, a plenty. There has been only one George Gershwin."

Sam H. Harris: "I shall always think of George Gershwin as one of the most valiant persons I have ever known. I never met anyone who seemed to enjoy life to the hilt as he did, or who gloried more in achievement. It was the game, more than the reward, that delighted him."

Eva Gauthier: "So Hail and Farewell to a great composer, pianist, painter, good friend, and a delightful host! They say 'Whom the gods love, die young.' He had more than his share of talent, and I hope the *Stairway to Paradise* was there to guide him on his way to the great beyond."

David Ewen: "I feel strongly that in *Porgy and Bess* Gersh-

Fragment of the jazz idiom, by M. A.

Mythology, by M. A.

win was disclosing new horizons as a composer of serious music. . . . It is this feeling which makes the sting of his passing so much more difficult."

Isamu Noguchi: "His deep-rooted appreciation of the artist behind art is nowhere better shown that in his interest in collecting their paintings. To him the painting was the artist, their work a study and a joy. He was forever trying to explain such things to his friends."

S. N. Behrman: "You get the sense of complete mastery, a complete authority—the most satisfactory feeling any artist can give you. I have seen Kreisler, Zimbalist, Auer, and Heifetz caught up in the heady surf that inundates a room the moment he strikes a chord. At the piano Gershwin takes on a new life, and so do his auditors."

Beverly Nichols: "Only by ragged words, by a mass of stage effects, by strident and jagged adjectives could one hope to recapture on the printed page the entangled and enticing rhythms which floated across the room when Gershwin played."

Merle Armitage: "George Gershwin possessed the love of Broadway, the admiration of the motion-picture industry, and the respect of the serious musical world; an unparalleled accomplishment. And he had one supreme quality, without which everything else would have availed little. He had style!"

Beryl Rubinstein, Carl Van Vechten, and Eva Gauthier were the *first* courageously to state their convictions that George Gershwin was a great composer. Their faith became a sustaining force in his life. Their perspicacity has been proved by events and developments.

In 1955 Louis Untermeyer published his *Makers of the Modern World*. Only four composers were mentioned: Wagner, Debussy, Stravinsky, and Gershwin.

6. Porgy and Bess

THE death of George made it imperative that I proceed with the production of *Porgy and Bess* as promised. Ira was extremely helpful. Rouben Mamoulian proved an indispensable man, for he came to Hollywood and became my chief adviser as he later whipped the company itself into shape, a masterly performance on the part of a director who had the qualities of a sorcerer.

The problems were immense. Arrangements had to be made with the Theatre Guild for our coast productions. Scenery, costumes, and props had to be built and acquired. Theaters had to be engaged all through the West, from Seattle and Portland and as far into the Southwest as Phoenix and Tucson. It was impossible to present such an expensive production just in Los Angeles and San Francisco; a much longer run was needed to refund the pre-production costs, including rehearsals.

Recruiting the company became my first thought, and we had a great deal of good fortune in finding most of the former company so enthused about an opportunity to play Gershwin's music drama again that many members of the cast actually turned down other offers, or took leave from engagements, in order to be with us. A young man who had been with the Theatre Guild performances, R. A. Wachsman, was engaged to handle the production details, the thousand-and-one comparatively small but all-important things without which a stage director cannot successfully work. He also knew all members of the company, which was a great asset, and he proved a good man.

The management end occupied my own time and thoughts as soon as we were assured that the important members of the company would join us. The question of the right man for the role of Porgy was first in my mind, as Todd Duncan had made a great success in the original production. In this respect George had been of great assistance, for he had helped me obtain Duncan for the two concerts given in February 1937. In consideration of my plans to produce *Porgy and Bess* the following year, George had written Duncan as follows:

March 16, 1937

DEAR TODD,

Just a little note to tell you what a great pleasure it was to have you come out to Los Angeles and sing at the two concerts. Your voice sounded better than ever. I'm sure you got a big kick out of receiving such a fine reception from such a distinguished audience as we had.

I hope Merle Armitage can manage to bring the entire opera out next season. He is definitely a superior impresario who does things well and I would love the West Coast to hear my opera as it was originally sung in New York.

Please extend my best wishes to Mrs. Duncan.

With kind regards,

Sincerely,

GEORGE GERSHWIN

Todd Duncan's respect and affection for George made my later invitation to sing Porgy a foregone conclusion, and Todd Duncan was the first to arrive for rehearsals in Los Angeles.

San Francisco was, of course, necessary to our plans. That

problem was solved by a protégé of mine who had recently established himself in that superb city. Paul Posz, a young man of good family, was enchanted with the theater and with music. He had asked to join me in some capacity, any capacity, several years before. The only unfilled position on my staff was that of head usher of the Philharmonic Auditorium, which I managed in addition to my other projects and activities. He made such an efficient and courteous head usher that I soon added the office of treasurer to his other duties. Then I took him with me to New York on one of my annual trips to engage, together with the late Gaetano Merola, the stars for our annual seasons of grand opera in San Francisco and Los Angeles. This gave Posz a broader understanding of the problems, for the concert and opera professions are largely made up of problems.

Posz was originally planning to present the artists whom I took across the continent each year in San Francisco, the Rosa Ponselles, Feodor Chaliapins, John Charles Thomases. But the opportunity to present *Porgy and Bess* to music-loving San Francisco gave Paul Posz a wonderful introductory year, and he made the most of it.

By the time we were in rehearsal, all large cities on the coast, and in Arizona and New Mexico, had signed up for this work. By the time the Los Angeles engagement was coming to a close the concert managers in Kansas City, Chicago, Detroit, Cincinnati, Pittsburgh, and Buffalo had asked for it, and theater managers in many other cities had wired for terms. By simply bridging the gap between Tucson and Denver, which would be simple, *Porgy and Bess*, my company, could confidently look forward to a national tour. Everyone was enthusiastic, for things could not have looked better.

Rouben Mamoulian, upon his return from Europe, following my strong appeal, consented to direct. Seven weeks were required to build the settings, including the massive realism of Catfish Row. The members of the company arrived three to four weeks before our opening date for intensive night-and-day rehearsals.

Among our major problems was the proper young man to play Sportin' Life, one of the trickiest bits of casting in show business. This role in the original production had been the special property of Bubbles of the team of Buck and Bubbles. But Bubbles asked a fee that would have satisfied a Hollywood motion-picture star. Our quest for a substitute was favored with great good luck. The day we "discovered" Avon Long, we knew we had our man. As he developed, we were astonished at his inventiveness. Avon Long has made Sportin' Life one of the most fascinatingly stylized and provocative characters in the American theater. When Cheryl Crawford produced the second revival of *Porgy and Bess* in the season 1942–43, Avon Long again played the role, pointing up every nuance of its sinister or roguish or hilariously blasphemous possibilities.

In addition to building the enormous sets, we designed and made every costume for the production, worked out on a chromatic scale plan giving life and vitality to the stage picture.

Motivating our efforts was my desire to make certain that we did not let George Gershwin down. That feeling was shared by every person in the cast and by the executives. It was therefore a great satisfaction to all of us when, following the first performances, dozens of Hollywood stars, theatrical personages, and others expert in the theater frankly expressed themselves as finding our performances much more satisfying and exciting than had been the original performances in New York. The company itself thought so. And that is not a criticism of the Theatre Guild, which had been most co-operative. We had the benefit of their experience.

A first performance, planned for Pasadena, was followed by eleven performances in Los Angeles at my theater (the Philharmonic Auditorium), three weeks at San Francisco's Curran Theatre, plus a series of performances in the principal cities of the West. But those last engagements were never played. Floods, engulfing all of California, began their terrifying havoc during the last week of the San Francisco run, and for more than seven days no trains moved.

Rouben Mamoulian had become a figure in Hollywood at the time of our *Porgy and Bess* engagement (1938) but Hollywood had never seen a Mamoulian-directed stage performance. There was great interest in what he would do. Actually, he was on the spot, as all the motion-picture executives and stars would attend these performances. I was very conscious of this. Mamoulian, knowing the terrific cost of the undertaking, realizing that in my eyes it was not a commercial venture, had promised his services gratis. This was a gesture which proves anew the generosity of theatrical people when they believe in a cause. I shall always be indebted to Mamoulian.

But my plans to give him ample time and a free hand were ironically frustrated. Because of a matinee of the Philharmonic Orchestra, we could not install our scenery and equipment until five o'clock the afternoon of our Los Angeles opening. The lighting, an important element in Mamoulian's direction, had required three days to accomplish in the original production. When our scenery was placed and electrical equipment installed, Mamoulian had barely *thirty minutes* to light our show. He was game and generous, and did his best with superlative results. Assisting him were Frances Herriott and Burton

The Playgoer

THE MAGAZINE IN THE THEATRE

MERLE ARMITAGE PRESENTS

GEORGE GERSHWIN'S

PORGY
& BESS

BY ARRANGEMENT WITH THE
THEATRE GUILD, NEW YORK

PHILHARMONIC
AUDITORIUM

Program cover by M. A.

McEvilly, two veterans of the original production who worked heroically for three strenuous weeks.

Everyone, including Alexander Steinert, our conductor, was exhausted. At ten minutes to eight the night we opened he suddenly recalled leaving his conductor's score in Pasadena, and the curtain was due to rise at half-past eight. With trepidation I dialed the number of Pasadena's Municipal Auditorium, where we had played the night before. The house, I knew, was dark. With sinking hope, I heard the phone ring for the thirteenth time, then someone took off the receiver.

"Hello," a dull voice responded. Apparently I had a janitor on the wire. Explaining with excruciating care who we were and what we wanted, I tried to make clear the importance of that score as well as its appearance.

"It's somewhere in the orchestra pit," I repeated over and over again.

"De place vhere de moositions sets is vut yu meens?" he finally asked, light beginning to dawn. I enthusiastically assured him.

"I look," said he. I waited an eternity before his voice was heard again. The book, he said, was in his hands. Instructing him to hold it until the police arrived and to give it to no one else, I got the Pasadena desk sergeant on the phone and told him the sad story. Could a police car pick up that score and bring it to us? Grumbling about my nerve, he instructed us to meet his car at the Pasadena city limits, on the Figueroa Bridge. An usher took my car and started north. Fifteen minutes later, as Steinert climbed into the pit, the score lay on the conductor's stand. The curtain went up on time.

Our only chance of breaking even on the tour was in the one-night *Porgy and Bess* engagements. On these contracts had been prorated the huge pre-production costs. When the disastrous floods prevented further movement, we were forced to close in San Francisco. It was impossible to liquidate fast enough to meet the final week's salaries of the company.

To inform the singers of this unavoidable truth was not an easy matter. We gave it considerable thought and finally decided that the straight, unadulterated truth would be the kindest, most effective means. But we expected trouble when, after the last performance, we assembled them on the stage of the Curran Theatre. The San Francisco manager, my friend Paul Posz, supported me. There were some "tough hombres" in the chorus. I was uncertain of many of the principals.

As circumstances leading to the final failure were related, there were audible groans of sympathy from the company, stars and chorus alike. "I'm in a most unfortunate position, my friends, I'm completely wiped out," I told them in closing.

Then occurred one of the most touching incidents of my career, a gesture on the part of those sympathetic and understanding Negroes which moved me profoundly. It was *my* misfortune, not theirs, which concerned them. Before I could leave the stage that night, completely surrounded by the company, who were bent on cheering me up, dozens of them diplomatically and generously offered loans from their meager savings.

There were factors of great consequence in these coast performances. Audiences, unaware of the critics' attitude in the Theatre Guild performances, were of course enthralled. But the great significance was the effect on Hollywood. The New York performances had been seen by few producers, writers, and directors of motion pictures. *Porgy and Bess* was just a name to most of them, although they had been mightily impressed by the two Gershwin concerts. The first-night audience was largely made up of the top Hollywood personalities, with a sprinkling of Beverly Hills, Bel-Air, and Brentwood socialites. They were simply stunned.

We had to hire three extra operators to handle the phone calls for reservations which broke like a dam and nearly inundated us. From then on and to the close of the engagement Hollywood responded as it never had before or since for a production in the theater. For the final performances in Los Angeles seats sold as high as fifty dollars each, as we had sold every seat in the auditorium five days before closing.

The name George Gershwin took on new significance to the men who handle the destinies of show business in America, and this had a great deal to do with the eventual production of a motion picture on the life of Gershwin.

San Francisco repeated this success; hundreds of persons from Los Angeles and vicinity made the thousand-mile trip to San Francisco and return, because they had been unable to obtain tickets for the first performances.

David Ewen in his *Journey to Greatness* said: "*Porgy and Bess* was an outstanding box-office success and one of the major artistic events in California that year." A correspondent for *Musical America* wrote: " ... The emphatic approbation of a star-studded first-night audience greeted *Porgy and Bess*."

7. Gershwin's Contemporaries

ALTHOUGH this is a book about George Gershwin, and although in my judgment he is unique, he is certainly not singular. To place him in juxtaposition with other American composers is necessary to an understanding of his time and environment, and to make no mention of other very distinguished Americans could be misunderstood. This country is now rich in men of superb talent for whom my admiration is of long standing.

My first contact with an American composer goes back to my Boston days when I heard the chamber music of Charles Martin Loeffler. Later I managed national tours of the very aristocratic combination of George Barrère's *Little Symphony* and Bolm's *Ballet Intime*, and idea of the late Catherine Bamman. Encountered here for the first time was the music of Charles Griffes, particularly the *White Peacock*. Although Griffes wrote in a somewhat European manner, with decided leanings toward Debussy, he was a strikingly talented man. His *Poem*, his colorful *Pleasure Dome of Kubla Khan*, his *Piano Sonata* as well as *White Peacock* are landmarks in American composition.

Anyone investigating the history of composition in this country will come to grips with a conservative group such as Daniel Gregory Mason, Deems Taylor, Charles Wakefield

Cadman, and Randall Thompson. Howard Hanson particularly has been an influence. John Alden Carpenter had a decidedly humorous outlook and, while influenced by both Debussy and Ravel, made some notable contributions with a delightful touch of jazz.

One of the most interesting and arresting men is Charles Ives. A daring and original New Englander, he is as American as are the lithographs of Currier and Ives. His instrumental works contain evocative, unorthodox harmonic and rhythmic devices of the highest inventive quality. He wrote these before Stravinsky or Schoenberg, not to mention Bartók, were known in this country. Ives is a man who will later be "discovered" as great and original. I came to know his music through my friend Edgar Varèse.

One of the most impressive contemporaries is Aaron Copland. Touring with Martha Graham and her company brought me into contact with his *Appalachian Spring*, a ballet suite so individual and rich that it stands up magnificently as a symphonic number. Having heard his *Billy the Kid* and *Rodeo* when managing the Lincoln Kirstein ballet organization, I knew that a powerful voice had come into the American music picture. Especially recommended is his *Lincoln Portrait* to which I was introduced by the conductor, Artur Rodzinsky. Copland has a very distinctive musical speech derived from his great interest in the work of Stravinsky, American jazz, folk songs, and from the Hebrew synagogue. He has wit, invention, and a brittle invigorating style without a trace of sentimentality.

Roy Harris is an important composer who at times is unnecessarily pretentious. But at his best, as in *Soliloquy and Dance* or the *passacaglia* of the *Piano Quintet,* Harris demonstrates his powers as a really original and powerful man. Some of his creations attain a primitive vitality that takes them almost to heroic grandeur, and he stands high in contemporary accomplishment.

William Schuman has a greater facility and expertness than Harris and he, too, has already gained a musical stature of great maturity. In his *Third Symphony*, for instance, the qualities of daring, emotional, and dynamic power are equaled by his rhythmic impact. He is capable of great lyric heights. Too little of his work is known to me for a full appreciation of it, but I can recall the magnificent score he provided for the ballet *Undertow*. Schuman certainly goes in the very first paragraph of American composers.

Virgil Thomson is a brilliant composer-critic, perhaps the most erudite and cosmopolitan of the new generation. The score he wrote for the film *The Plow That Broke the Plains* will undoubtedly become an American classic. His handling of folk melodies is superb, notably the "Cattle" episode. Stimulating musical cocktails are his initial *Bugles and Birds* sketch of Picasso, and the *Percussion Piece*, reminiscent of Chinese *objets d'art*. His *Cantabile for Strings* is impressive.

But his most delightful and provocative work is *Four Saints in Three Acts*, with text by Gertrude Stein. Surrealistic, it is gay but haunting. Using Negro singers and actors, the work is certainly one of the most original fantasies written by any composer in our time. *Four Saints* has been performed in Hartford, New York, and Chicago under the auspices of the Friends and Enemies of Modern Music.

Varèse in my opinion is a giant and will take his place with the group that posterity will elect to the highest honors. Leopold Stokowski and the Philadelphia Orchestra introduced him to this country where he has always been an influence with the intellectuals and the musically advanced. For a new musical experience, hear his *Amériques, Ionisation, Intégrales,* or his latest, *Déserts.* He is certainly one of the significant influences in contemporary music, powerful, experimental, and courageous.

Other extremely important composers of the United States are Samuel Barber, whose opera *Vanessa* has been performed at the Metropolitan Opera, Walter Piston, David Diamond, Lukas Foss, Norman dello Joio, George Antheil, Roger Sessions, and Wallingford Riegger.

But the man whose career most closely parallels that of George Gershwin is Leonard Bernstein. Like Gershwin, he ranges from Broadway shows to symphonic compositions. He seems equally at home in resources and abilities. Unlike George, however, his career has been graced by a group of sophisticated and mature critics who have evaluated him on his merits, whether these qualities have been exhibited in ballet performances, shows, or with symphony orchestras. Where George went on from his earlier works to write his supreme opus, *Porgy and Bess,* Bernstein has progressed to the pinnacle of musicianship as the permanent conductor of the New York Philharmonic Orchestra. But his career has not been without members of the raised-eyebrow set proclaiming their dismay as he has tackled assignments of which they disapproved. In the January 18, 1958, issue of *The New Yorker,* Robert Rice regales us with some interesting sidelights on this. Without quoting him directly, the substance is that Koussevitzky really gave him a Dutch-uncle dressing down for wasting his time and talents on a Broadway musical. Other purists and reactionaries began to regard Bernstein with a fishy eye when his picture appeared in magazines such as *Harper's Bazaar,* and when he was quoted or mentioned by the various columnists, particularly by Leonard Lyons. One of these august gentlemen said it really pained him very much to realize that, after all, Bernstein apparently wanted to be a world personality, like Frank Sinatra, for instance! Bernstein used to sit at the feet of eminent men, most of whom were distinguished musicians. They also found it very hard to understand when a great conductor like Bernstein was besieged by bobby-soxers, and over-enthusiastic autograph hunters. Their European minds and training just revolted against this evidence of popular acclaim. Robert Rice thinks, however, that this sort of attitude on the part of Bernstein's overcautious friends is diminishing. As a matter of fact, they are finding that this youthful and fiery conductor is bringing more people to the world of great music, and that his superb and ever-present showmanship may do the venerable Philharmonic a real service. He is certainly making public performances of the classics more attractive and interesting to more people.

And in the world of the theater and popular music there are famous and successful names who were contemporaries of George Gershwin. Jerome Kern, Cole Porter, Irving Berlin, Arthur Schwartz, Richard Rodgers, Vernon Duke, Allie Wrubel, Victor Young, to name some of the great figures, as well as W. C. Handy and Duke Ellington.

As a postscript to this review of George Gershwin and his contemporaries there must be at least a paragraph about the indefatigable Henry Cowell. The honor fell to me to manage his very first public appearance back in 1920. His soft-spoken approach to all problems in life, including that of securing an audience for an unknown and eccentric composer, completely misled me. For when this modest young man walked out on the stage before a very sizable audience and began his *Tides of Monanon*, played with entire forearm in "tone-clusters," the effect was orchestral, bewildering, and wonderful. Through the years it has been interesting to watch Cowell, and his zest and enthusiasm for sound and for experimenting are as great as ever. His home contains, in addition to the ever-present piano, Persian drums, oriental flutes, and many other exotic instruments, including four resonant Pyrex bowls. He has lectured all over the world as well as in America and is a sometime teacher at Columbia University and the New School. Cowell is a contemporary whom George Gershwin probably never heard of, but in his quiet way he has set in motion many brilliant ideas and given a very vigorous shove toward opening the door to new musical experience.

(NOTE. Ira read this in manuscript, and wrote me the following: "Henry Cowell. George knew him very well. One night I was present when Cowell played many of his compositions at George's home. I remember the title of one I particularly liked: *Banshee!* You might add something just discovered. In the latest *Britannica* under "Music," the only American-born composer on the page of twenty-five portraits from Palestrina on is George Gershwin.)

Against this chorus of brilliant men George Gershwin found himself organized in another, and a very different, direction. His music has penetrated to the remote corners of the earth; because he was true to his own instincts and concepts, his musical convictions have achieved world stature.

Time and many other factors have handsomely established the music of George Gershwin. Facts are available in convincing abundance. Popularity is a capricious yardstick, for it can also be ruinous. Popularity was a direct factor in the non-acceptance of Gershwin as a serious composer. This fever having run its course, Gershwin emerges as a major voice. Symphony-orchestra conductors, a knowing and a cautious group, have voted overwhelmingly for him, as have audiences. On

New patterns in music, by M. A.

MERLE ARMITAGE PRESENTS GEORGE GERSHWIN
WITH THE PHILHARMONIC ORCHESTRA OF LOS
ANGELES, ALEXANDER SMALLENS CONDUCTING,
IN AN ALL GERSHWIN PROGRAM ASSISTED BY TODD
DUNCAN ORIGINAL "PORGY" OF THE NEW YORK CAST AND MARGUERITE CHAPMAN
SUPPORTED BY A NEGRO CHORUS OF SIXTEEN VOICES

P · R · O · G · R · A · M

1. AN AMERICAN IN PARIS CONDUCTED BY ALEXANDER SMALLENS

2 CONCERTO IN F CONDUCTED BY ALEXANDER SMALLENS
GEORGE GERSHWIN, PIANO SOLOIST

I N T E R M I S S I O N

3. EXCERPTS FROM "PORGY AND BESS" WITH TODD DUNCAN
MISS CHAPMAN
NEGRO CHORUS AND PHILHARMONIC ORCHESTRA CONDUCTED BY GEORGE GERSHWIN

(A) PRELUDE
SUMMERTIME } . . MARGUERITE CHAPMAN AND CHORUS
(B) TRAIN SONG
. . MARGUERITE CHAPMAN AND CHORUS
(C) I GOT PLENTY OF NUTTIN
. . . . TODD DUNCAN AND CHORUS

(D) DUET—BESS YOU IS MY WOMAN NOW
MARGUERITE CHAPMAN & TODD DUNCAN
(E) STORM MUSIC . . . . . . ORCHESTRA
(F) BUZZARD SONG
(G) SPIRITUAL—O LORD I'M ON MY WAY
. . . . . TODD DUNCAN AND CHORUS

4. C U B A N   O V E R T U R E CONDUCTED BY ALEXANDER SMALLENS

5. R H A P S O D Y   I N   B L U E SMALLENS, CONDUCTOR
GERSHWIN, SOLOIST

PHILHARMONIC ORCHESTRA BY ARRANGEMENT · WITH
SOUTHERN CALIFORNIA SYMPHONY ASSOCIATION
MEMBERS OF THE CHORUS TRAINED BY BELLE RILEY
STEINWAY PIANO BY THE COURTESY OF BARKER· BROS.
RAY DAVIDSON, PUBLICITY DIRECTOR · PAUL POSZ, ASSOCIATE MANAGER
WITH MERLE ARMITAGE · J. HOWARD JOHNSON, RADIO

Program designed by M. A.

symphony programs in Europe as in America, Gershwin is a three-to-one favorite. A new generation of sophisticated critics, who understand the fundamental contribution of jazz, has given Gershwin a full measure of recognition. The general acceptance of *Porgy and Bess* as the significant music drama of our time has clinched the argument. This is the dominant theme of the final chapter of this book, the history of *Porgy and Bess*. The masses and the understanding audiences have accepted it with equal enthusiasm. Nothing written by an American approaches it in basic originality, humanity, construction, and invention. It stands alone. In this verdict, audiences and critics of the world agree.

Gershwin's music for the theater and his songs are yet regarded in a class by themselves. No longer do they inhibit full recognition of his serious works.

And nothing destroys unworthy music as does repetition. Gershwin's music has met this supreme test. No other music has been presented to so many concert and theater audiences, or on so many radio and television programs, or in so many motion pictures and recordings. Yet the demand for Gershwin music in every category is steadily rising.

The unseen results are just as important. A new freedom has come for composers, for Gershwin has opened the most inaccessible doors. Without question the first half of this century belongs to George Gershwin.

His was a hard road which he took at terrific speed.

But he definitely arrived.

I can see him as he carefully looks about at the company he has joined. Over there is the rotund, handsome Bach, and here the white mane of Liszt. Farther away, the frowning, suffering Beethoven, and the delicate, romantic profile of Chopin. Palestrina is having an *apéritif* with the brilliant, youthful Mozart. The aesthete, Debussy, is slightly withdrawn, as he listens to the languorous music of the stars. Wagner, far to the right, is attempting to get the attention of Jove.

And I can see George, relaxed at last. He gives them all his wonderful smile, a smile of joy and humility. For he has just seen a piano as it emerges from a cloud.

8. The History of
Porgy and Bess

THE mere facts of the history of *Porgy and Bess* need no embellishment; its saga is without a counterpart in the whole field of opera or music drama. Beginning as the story of a humble cripple in Charleston, it moves with accelerated speed. Its momentum carried it to the great cities of the world.

In 1926, George Gershwin read the DuBose Heyward novel, *Porgy*, the story of a Negro beggar of Charleston's Catfish Row. George was impressed, believing he had at last found the proper vehicle for his long-considered operatic plans.

He immediately wrote to Heyward, and their meeting in Charleston resulted in an agreement to make an opera, using the story of *Porgy*. Neither George nor Heyward was free to proceed with their plans. Gershwin had commitments that prevented taking on such an arduous assignment, while Heyward and his wife Dorothy were to proceed with a dramatization of the book. As a play *Porgy* was produced by the Theatre Guild in 1927.

In 1933 Gershwin began working on the opera. Because Heyward liked to work only in the South and Gershwin was tied to New York by a radio contract, most of the collaboration from November 1933 to July 1934 was done by mail. Heyward's main problem was cutting the dialogue of the play by about 40 per cent so that the music might fit, and it was agreed that he would write the scenes and lyrics first and then send them North to Gershwin. After receiving them, the composer and his lyric-writing brother Ira—who had joined the venture a few months after it began—would, in the words of DuBose Heyward, "get at the piano, pound, wrangle, swear, burst into weird snatches of song, and eventually emerge with a polished lyric."

In December 1933 and also in January 1934, George Gershwin went to Charleston for brief visits, and in April 1934, the librettist spent a short time at the Gershwin home in New York. For the most part, they worked together smoothly. Rather than objecting to the intrusion of brother Ira, Heyward welcomed the opportunity to work with a lyricist with so much theatrical experience. The main difference of opinion arose over the use of recitative, which the composer insisted upon keeping in the opera, and which the librettist would have preferred to eliminate in favor of spoken dialogue.

The lyric credits were divided almost equally between Ira Gershwin and Heyward. The more sophisticated words to Sportin' Life's songs—"It Ain't Necessarily So" and "There's a Boat Dat's Leavin' Soon for New York"—were Ira's work. The more simple and native emotions—"Summertime," "Buzzard Song," "It Takes a Long Pull to Get There," "A Woman Is a Sometime Thing," and "My Man's Gone Now"—were expressed by Heyward. Although "Bess, You Is My Woman Now," "I Loves You, Porgy," "A Red-Headed Woman," and "Oh, I Can't Sit Down" were written mostly by Ira, he freely admits that the ideas came from Heyward, and that many words and phrases were taken directly from Heyward's libretto. "I Got Plenty o' Nuttin' " was the only song whose music was written before the lyrics, for which both Heyward and Ira Gershwin received credit.

In July 1934 George Gershwin rented a cottage for two months on Folly Island, about ten miles off Charleston. This was adjacent to James Island, where there was a large population of primitive Gullah Negroes, and Gershwin went there often to observe the people and to take part in their singing and "shouting" at revival meetings. He worked on the score until about mid-April 1935, with the complete orchestrations taking him until September of that year. In all, the project took Gershwin eleven months to compose and nine months to orchestrate, with the published vocal and piano score running to 559 pages and the orchestrations taking 700. The working title had been *Porgy*, but when the manuscript was finished, Heyward suggested calling it *Porgy and Bess* to avoid confusion with the play. Gershwin also liked the new title because it was in the operatic tradition of *Samson et Dalila, Tristan und Isolde* and *Pelléas et Mélisande.*

Both Gershwin and Heyward were given a free hand by the Theatre Guild in the matter of production staff and cast. Rehearsals started August 26, 1935, under the direction of Rouben Mamoulian, who had staged the original *Porgy*, and Alexander Smallens, a symphonic conductor, chosen as musical director. The principals in the cast were coached by Alexander Steinert, formerly with the Russian Opera Company. The settings were designed by Sergei Soudeikine. The choral director was Eva Jessye, and Russel Crouse was press representative.

The cast had to use virtually unknown singers in the leading roles, as there were few Negroes at that time with professional operatic experience. Neither Todd Duncan (Porgy) nor Anne Brown (Bess) had ever appeared on the professional stage before. The role for Sportin' Life went to John W. Bubbles, and his vaudeville partner, Ford L. Buck, played Mingo. George Harvey (Maria) was the only one in the cast who had appeared in the original *Porgy*. Other performers included Helen Dowdy as Dily and the Strawberry Woman, Ruby Elzy as Serena, Abbie Mitchell as Clara, Warren Coleman as Crown, Edward Matthews as Jake, and J. Rosamond Johnson as Frazier. One of the chief problems was to teach the cast, made up for the most part of Northern well-educated Negroes, how to sing in a primitive Southern Negro dialect.

BOSTON AND NEW YORK (1935)

The world première of *Porgy and Bess*—billed as "An American Folk Opera"—took place at the Colonial Theatre, Boston, on September 30, 1935. Although it was considered somewhat long, both audiences and critics were enthusiastic, with Serge Koussevitzky pronouncing it "a great advance in American opera." Before it reached New York, about thirty minutes were pared, resulting in the elimination of "Buzzard Song," "I Ain't Got No Shame," and a dance at the beginning of the opera.

The Broadway opening at the Alvin Theatre, October 10, 1935, exactly eight years after *Porgy*, marked the first time that a theatrical work with an all-Negro cast had played to a $4.40 top.

Shortly after the opening, the first "authorized" recordings were made by Victor under the supervision of the composer. Called *Highlights from Porgy and Bess*, the selections were sung by Lawrence Tibbett and Helen Jepson in an album consisting of four 12-inch 78-rpm records. Alexander Smallens and Nathaniel Shilkret conducted.

In an attempt to keep the show going, the top price was lowered in December to $3.30, but even so it lasted only one hundred twenty-four performances. While this would be impressive compared to the number of times a work is performed during one season at the Metropolitan, it did not make a financial success, but lost all of its $70,000 investment. After its stay in New York, *Porgy and Bess* took to the road for two months, visiting Philadelphia, Pittsburgh, Chicago, Detroit, and Washington, D.C. Alexander Steinert was musical director for the tour.

On July 11, 1937, while working in Hollywood on the score for the film, *The Goldwyn Follies*, George Gershwin died of a brain tumor. Shortly afterward the New York *Times* editorialized, "*Porgy and Bess* is utterly innocent of elemental tragedy or anything of real dramatic import." Possibly aware of that estimate, Gershwin's executors appraised the opera as of "nominal value." *Rhapsody in Blue* was valued at $20,000.

Porgy and Bess was presented on the coast by Merle Armitage. Opening in the Philharmonic Auditorium in Los Angeles, it ran in that theater for three highly successful weeks, with one night at the Pasadena Auditorium, and then three capacity weeks at the Curran Theatre in San Francisco. These performances were staged by Rouben Mamoulian and conducted by Alexander Steinert. Avon Long made his debut with this company as Sportin' Life, and henceforth was identified with many other performances. The scenery and costumes, designed by Merle Armitage, were produced on the coast.

The importance of these performances, beyond their artistic merit which was superb, was the interest aroused in the motion-picture industry. Hollywood studio heads, directors, producers, writers, actors, and actresses were stunned by the impact of *Porgy and Bess*. "It won," reported a correspondent for *Musical America*, "the emphatic approbation of a star-sprinkled first-night audience." It was the major artistic event in California that year. Near the end of the San Francisco run, California was visited by the worst flood in its history. The railways could not operate anywhere in the state for eight days. Although all major cities in the West had asked for the Armitage performances of *Porgy and Bess,* and it could have run indefinitely, the company was forced to close at the end of the San Francisco season.

DECCA RECORDS PRODUCTION (1940)

In one of the first attempts to record a musical with members of its original cast, Decca recorded selections from *Porgy and Bess* in May 1940, featuring Todd Duncan, Anne Brown, and the Eva Jessye Choir with Alexander Smallens conducting. After the 1942 revival, a second volume was released, containing other numbers sung by the principals and others in the company. Both collections, totaling fourteen pieces, have been combined on one 12-inch long-playing record, DL 8042.

As part of the regular season at her Maplewood, New Jersey, theater, Cheryl Crawford, who had been an assistant stage manager during the original production of the play *Porgy,* revived *Porgy and Bess* with Todd Duncan, Anne Brown, and the other members of the cast assembled for the Merle Armitage West Coast production in 1938. Under the direction of Robert Ross, and with Alexander Smallens as musical director, it played to capacity during its week-long run beginning October 13, 1941. Virgil Thomson, covering the production for the New York *Herald Tribune,* reversed his earlier judgment by now observing, "The score has musical distinction and popular appeal." So great was the reception that Miss Crawford decided to produce *Porgy and Bess* on Broadway, in association with John Wildberg.

But she was determined that this time it would be financially successful, which it had not been when first presented in 1935. Instead of an "opera" or even a "folk opera" (as in 1935), it was listed in the ads as "George Gershwin's *Porgy and Bess.*"

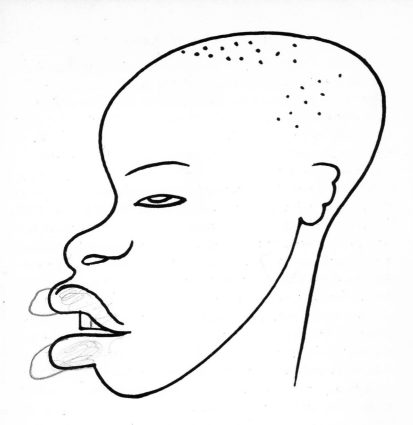

Gullah negro, by Covarrubias

The original cast of eighty was cut almost in half, and the orchestra was reduced from forty-two to twenty-seven pieces. Most of the recitative was eliminated, thus shortening the work considerably. The cast and the production staff were the same as in Maplewood, with Herbert Andrews receiving credit for the scenery, and Paul du Pont, then an assistant stage manager, supervising the costumes.

After three weeks in Boston—where it earned its entire investment of $16,500—*Porgy and Bess* opened at the Majestic Theatre in New York on January 22, 1942. This time, in contrast to the mixed critical reception of the original production, it was greeted with enthusiasm by press and public. "Classic" was the word used to describe it by Richard Watts, Jr., in the *Herald Tribune* and Wolcott Gibbs in *The New Yorker*. "See it if you see nothing else," urged Louis Kronenberger in *PM*. "Belongs on your 'must' list," advised John Mason Brown in the *World-Telegram*. Later the Music Critics Circle designated it as the most significant musical revival of the year. At a price scale of $.55 to $2.75, the public responded eagerly, and the production lasted until September 26, 1942. Its run of 286 performances was the longest of any other theatrical revival in New York at that time.

Porgy and Bess toured forty-seven cities in the United States and Toronto, Canada, from September 28, 1942, to April 8, 1944, when it ended its travels at the New York City Center. For the road company, Etta Moten succeeded Anne Brown, and during the tour Mr. Duncan was replaced by William Franklin. In March 1944, Buck and Bubbles returned to play their original roles.

By this time the fame of *Porgy and Bess* had spread around the world. Its European première was held at the Danish Royal Opera in Copenhagen, March 27, 1943, during the German occupation. With a translation by Holger Bech and an all-Danish cast, it was one of the most popular productions ever offered in Denmark, and played twenty-two times during the season. It was withdrawn only after the Nazis threatened to bomb the theater if another performance were given. In a way *Porgy and Bess* became a symbol of Danish resistance. Every time the Germans would broadcast a victory communiqué over the Danish radio, the underground would cut in with a recording of "It Ain't Necessarily So." It returned to the repertory in 1945, and continued to be one of the most successful offerings until difficulties with the Gershwin estate in 1952 forced it to be withdrawn. From time to time Anne Brown and Todd Duncan have joined the company in their original roles.

On May 14, 1945, *Porgy and Bess* was performed in Moscow by the Stanislavsky Players to the accompaniment of a piano and drums. There it won the praise of composer Dimitri Shostakovitch, who compared Gershwin with Moussorgsky and Borodin. In June of that year it was performed as part of the annual Zurich Festival of Music. It was first heard in Sweden at the Lyriskateatern in Gothenburg on February 10, 1948, and later played the Oscarsteatern in Stockholm on April 1, 1949. In the fall of 1950, *Porgy and Bess* entered the regular repertory of the Zurich Stadttheater. In its German translation by Ralph Benatzsky, although it has always been given a production of great dignity, visiting Americans were amused to see the members of the cast covered with blue make-up, or to hear an aria such as "Bess, You Is My Woman Now," being sung as *"Bess, du bist meine frau jetzt."*

The next major—but strictly aural—version of *Porgy and Bess* was a three-record set (SL-162) released by Columbia Records in September 1951. This is the most complete production available on long-playing records, and features Lawrence Winters as Porgy, Camilla Williams as Bess, Avon Long as Sportin' Life, and Inez Matthews as Serena, with the orchestra conducted by Lehman Engel. Some of the words and lyrics have been changed slightly by Ira Gershwin, and such sound effects as footsteps, a fight, and the rattle of dice can be heard.

Porgy and Bess has now become internationally recognized as one of the greatest musical works, and probably the most enduring American music ever conceived—as a result of its recent stage production by Blevins Davis and Robert Breen.

Playing in most cases for just a few days to audiences limited by theater capacities, the George Gershwin musical drama went on tour of twenty-nine countries to enjoy enormous success and acclaim. The greatest opera house in the world, La Scala of Milan, presented it for a whole week—a unique recognition.

Since its first performance on October 10, 1935, *Porgy and Bess* has steadily increased in reputation. The exciting potential of the music drama is only being realized. The opportunity for movement and color, scope and intensity, narrative and drama demanded future development on the motion-picture screen.

The stage conception of *Porgy and Bess* by Robert Breen—for the Everyman Opera production—approached it from a *theater* rather than a conventional *opera* or *musical-comedy* point of view. The original production in 1935 was staged as an opera, as were the Merle Armitage performances. The Cheryl Crawford production in 1942 was in the musical-comedy vein—dialogue punctuated by musical numbers. The new directorial concept was one of unity and cohesiveness in the entire production—acting, dancing, singing, scenic and costume designing, lighting, orchestral approach, atmosphere, and timing—all blended harmoniously and complementing the whole. It would realize for the first time the "mass rhythms" DuBose Heyward wrote about in 1927.

Two musical passages, the "Buzzard Song" and "I Ain't Got No Shame," written but never performed, except in the Boston engagement, were presented on the stage. The "Buzzard Song" was woven into the final scene rather than its original place in the first act. The choral passages and recitative cut from the 1942 revival were restored. Stage waits were speeded up. The show was given in two acts rather than three.

From the original production in 1935 and the revival in 1942 came Alexander Smallens as musical director and Eva Jessye as choral director. Wolfgang Roth designed the settings; Jed Mace did the costumes; Samuel Matlowsky was the new assistant musical director. The producers, Blevins Davis and Robert Breen, had considerable experience in presenting American works abroad. Breen, who was director, first interested the Department of State in International Exchange of Theater, in his capacity as executive director of ANTA (American National Theater and Academy) from 1946 through 1951.

The new *Porgy and Bess* opened in Dallas, Texas, at the State Fair Auditorium on June 9, 1952. Leontyne Price and Urylee Leonardos alternated as Bess; William Warfield and LeVern Hutcherson alternated as Porgy; and Lorenzo Fuller played Sportin' Life. Helen Dowdy repeated her original roles of Lily and the Strawberry Woman; Georgia Burke played Maria; Helen Colbert was Clara; and John McCurry played big Crown. John Rosenfeld, dean of culture in the Southwest, reported in the Dallas *Morning News:* "The crowds gave the loudest and longest ovation ever heard at a summer musical performance." The box-office gross of $93,000 for fourteen performances set a record for the theater.

Cab Calloway took over the role of Sportin' Life at the next engagement, the Civic Opera House in Chicago. It was originally planned that he should have the role, but because of previous commitments he was not ready to open in Dallas. The Chicago writers used adjectives like "exciting," "memorable," "overpowering."

The critics in Pittsburgh were impressed. "One of the theater-going events of a lifetime . . . electric and pulsating theater, the kind that comes along once in a decade—perhaps in a generation," said Karl Krug in the Pittsburgh *Sun-Telegraph*. "Nobody can possibly say now that *Porgy and Bess* doesn't belong to the ages," wrote Harold V. Cohen in the Pittsburgh *Post-Gazette*. "An enduring monument to the genius of the late George Gershwin," reported Kaspar Monahan in the Pittsburgh *Press*.

In Washington, D.C., President Harry S. Truman attended the opening-night performance. One of the most authoritative critical voices in the United States, Richard L. Coe, wrote in the Washington *Post and Times Herald*, "This is a brilliant revival. That it will be a pleasure to American audiences for years to come was clear from the opening's stunning impression on a packed house." Coe was able to testify personally to these words when many months later his paper sent him to cover the opening of *Porgy and Bess* at La Scala Opera House in Milan. The Washington *Evening Star*'s Jay Carmody called the performance "one of democracy's historic moments."

The impact was such that *Porgy and Bess* was shipped off to Europe under the auspices of the State Department and ANTA, delaying a limited engagement at the Metropolitan

Opera House in New York scheduled for September 3, 1952. The first European performance was given at the Volksoper in Vienna on September 7, 1952. The ovation lasted thirty minutes, led by the President of Austria and United States High Commissioner, Llewellyn Thompson. The Vienna *Arbeiter Zeitung* said, "This company is the best ambassador for America." "There was curtain after curtain to give the singers of the other side of the Atlantic an opportunity to receive the audience's enthusiastic signs of gratitude which came straight from their hearts," declared the *Wiener Kurier*. "A great success with all the earmarks of a sensation," reported the *Neues Oesterreich*. Max Graf wrote in *Die Weltpresse*, "There can be no truer theater, no better company."

Porgy and Bess went to Berlin's Titania Palast on September 17, as part of a month-long Cultural Festival. At the end of the première performance, Robert Breen recorded twenty-nine minutes of applause by stop watch. The twenty-one curtain calls were not the ordinary sort. Members of the audience called out their praises to individual members of the cast as they took their bows. Critical discussion centered around whether *Porgy and Bess* was really an opera. There was no question of its impact. *Der Abend* called it "A new sensation"; *Die Neue Zeitung*, "A masterpiece"; *Telegraf*, "Fascinating, modern, explosive music"; *Der Tag*, "A revelation"; *Die Welt*, "No doubt the further travels will be more of a triumphant procession than a tour."

This last view could hardly be a more accurate description of the London and Paris engagements. The Stoll Theatre engagement, beginning in London on October 9, turned away nine hundred people the first day. A three-week run was extended to four months. London drama critics voted *Porgy and Bess* the best musical of the season. J. C. Trewin in the *Il-*

lustrated London News described it as "an urgently exciting spectacle"; Felix Aprahamian (*Sunday Times*) praised it as "The most animated and coordinated spectacle to be seen in London today"; Kenneth Tynan in the *Standard*, "A breast-beating, heart-pounding show"; W. A. Darlington (*Telegraph*), "The impact is completely shattering"; Alan Dent (*Picture Post*), "The most stunning event of the theatrical year."

The day after *Porgy and Bess* opened at Paris' Théâtre de l'Empire on February 16, 1953, the headline in *Le Figaro* read, "All Paris Was in Charleston Last Night." At seven dollars for top-priced tickets, the folk opera played to standing room only at the two-thousand-seat theater. *The New Yorker's* correspondent, Janet Flanner, observed, "It has achieved a triumphant success with the French such as is rarely enjoyed here. The reviewers were so phenomenal in their praise that several of them pointed out how extraordinary their reactions were." "Triumph" and "masterpiece" were the words used in the reviews in *Libération, France-Soir, Le Parisien, Franc-Tireur,* and *Paris Comoedia.*

Porgy and Bess finally returned home for its long-anticipated New York debut, opening on March 10 at the Ziegfeld Theatre. The critics gave overwhelming praise to the production and the cast, substantially the same, with Porgy played alternately by LeVern Hutcherson, Leslie Scott, and Irving Barnes. Brooks Atkinson in the *Times* called it, "All Gershwin and all gold." Walter Kerr in the *Herald Tribune* said it was "the most restless, urgent, and shatteringly explosive production of the Gershwin masterpiece." John Chapman wrote in the *Daily News*, "A work of art"; Richard Watts, Jr., in the *Post* called it, "One of the glories of the popular American musical theater"; William Hawkins in the *World Tele-*

gram and Sun said it "reveals stature and might far beyond anything it seemed to have in the past"; John McClain called it "lusty and lustrous" in the *Journal American*; Wolcott Gibbs in *The New Yorker* thought it "just about the most exciting thing in New York"; Irving Kolodin of the *Saturday Review* believed it to be "just about the most satisfying performance I have ever seen"; in *Cue Magazine*, John Keating hailed *Porgy and Bess* as "the most impressive single exhibit of the season. As staged by Robert Breen, it has a crackling excitement and a larger-than-life humanity which sets it over anything else the theater had to offer"; George Jean Nathan declared, "There is small question that it is in many respects the best achievement thus far in distinctive American opera."

When the New York run concluded on November 28 after a total of 305 performances, the company set out on its nationwide tour. Starting on December 1, 1953, in Philadelphia, *Porgy and Bess* played eighteen cities in the United States and Canada. There were return engagements in Washington, D.C., Pittsburgh, Chicago, and Toronto, as well as visits to Richmond, Cincinnati, St. Louis, Kansas City, Minneapolis, Detroit, Cleveland, Columbus, Denver, San Francisco, Los Angeles, Boston, and Montreal, concluding on September 18, 1954.

Everyman Opera decided on a second trip to Europe for *Porgy and Bess* on the basis of an invitation to appear as the final attraction of the Venice Bienelle, the seventeenth International Festival of Contemporary Music. Tickets sold for fifteen dollars at the Teatro La Fenice for the four performances beginning on September 22, 1954. A second Paris run had also been planned, beginning on September 30 for nine and one-half weeks. The role of Bess was being played by Irene Williams, Gloria Davy, and Fredye Marshall. Lorenzo Fuller,

James Attles, and Earl Jackson alternated in the role of Sportin' Life. Later on this tour, Martha Flowers and Ethel Ayler took on the role of Bess.

Official interest abroad had grown so in *Porgy and Bess* that President Eisenhower wrote to Blevins Davis: "You and your distinguished company are making a real contribution to the kind of understanding between peoples that alone can bring mutual respect and trust. You are, in a real sense, ambassadors of the arts." Whereupon the Department of State and ANTA requested the company to make a tour of the Middle East, beginning with Yugoslavia and ending in Naples, partially underwritten to the extent of $285,000.

The company traveled by train from Paris to Zagreb, Yugoslavia, opening on December 11 to a tumultuously cheering audience. Eager crowds kept an all-night vigil in the hope of getting tickets to the performances in Belgrade at the Théâtre de l'Opéra beginning on December 16. The Yugoslavian capital exploded with enthusiasm, the opening-night audience cheering wildly and throwing flowers. A government official remarked, "Only a psychologically mature people could have put this on the stage."

Egypt, the Théâtre Mohamed Aly in Alexandria and the Théâtre de l'Opéra in Cairo, saw *Porgy and Bess* next. The eight performances in the nation's capital were attended by 6,750 persons from January 7–12, 1955. Most critics were wildly enthusiastic, a few were lukewarm, but it scored a decided hit with the audiences.

Excitement mounted as the company reached Athens, Greece, for its engagement at the Royal National Theatre beginning on January 17. Wherever *Porgy and Bess* was to go, a very vigorous black market in tickets sprang into operation. In Athens, for example, Breen discovered that none of the students or young people were able to see the performances because of the prices. A special student matinee was arranged at lower prices. Tickets for this "student matinee" went on the black market, and Breen doubts if there was a student in the house. All this was in the face of a wave of anti-American feeling brought on by uprisings in Cyprus.

The reception in Israel was, if possible, even more enthusiastic. In honor of the company, a hundred and fifty trees were planted in the Herzl forest. At the first performance on January 26, the Soviet Ambassador remarked to Mrs. Ira Gershwin, "You know, if only *we* had *Porgy and Bess* how we'd send it around!" By January 30, closing night, the fever had mounted so to see *Porgy and Bess* at the Habimah Theatre in Tel Aviv that four hundred people actually broke through the glass in the front door and sat in the aisles to see the last twenty minutes.

To entertain United States personnel at the Nouasseur Air Depot in Casablanca, the troupe was flown almost three thousand miles from Tel Aviv for a single concert performance on January 31.

The Gran Teatro de Liceo and later the Windsor Palace were the homes for the *Porgy and Bess* engagement in Barcelona, Spain, from February 3–13. *Destino* called it, "The best thing seen in Barcelona for twenty years." *Solidaridad Nacional* observed, "Gershwin's music puts no limits on races and frontiers."

An Italian presentation began on February 15 in four cities, Naples, Milan, Genoa, and Florence. Without a doubt, the engagement at La Scala in Milan was the high point of the entire tour for the company—and the high point historically. It was the first time that Teatro alla Scala (founded in 1778) had ever presented a single opera for a full week; the first time an American company had ever played there; and the first time that the rule against applause during a new work was ever broken. With tickets sold out days in advance, the management of La Scala sought to extend the company's stay for another week or two. *L'Unità* referred to *Porgy and Bess* as "among the masterworks of the lyric theater."

In Lausanne, Switzerland, *Porgy and Bess* once again had to prove itself in the face of anti-American feelings, this time because of new regulations concerning the import of Swiss watches. A relatively small city, Lausanne had an extended engagement from March 16–23. After Marseilles, France, the company returned to Italy for performances in Turin and Rome. Because the Teatro dell'Opera was unavailable in Rome, it played a music hall, Teatro Quattro Fontane, from April 21–May 14. The pattern of success continued, with three final European engagements in Zurich, Switzerland, Brussels, and Antwerp, Belgium, concluding on June 30.

The United States Department of State now set a new "target area" for *Porgy and Bess*, Latin America, increasing its expenditure in aid to $400,000. From July 7 to October 25, 1955, the company visited the major cities of South and Central America. Because of shorter engagements and elaborate setting and lighting requirements, double sets of scenery and electrical equipment were carried, so that preparations could be under way one stop ahead.

The complete Latin-American tour covered more than 20,000 air miles. Of the estimated 170,000 persons who saw *Porgy and Bess* during this part of the tour, probably not more than a tenth could understand English. Yet, as previously, the show was greeted warmly wherever it went. In Rio de Janeiro, Brazil, where the show opened, the newspaper *Ultima*

G. G., a salute! from P. & B.

Hora, declared that "the spectacle deserves all the great applause it received."

Porgy and Bess played São Paulo, Brazil, and Montevideo, Uruguay. During the appearance in Buenos Aires, Argentina, at the Teatro Astral from August 3 to 21, the dictator Perón was overthrown. For a time no one was certain who was responsible for transportation of the sets. The company went on to Santiago, Chile; Lima, Peru; Bogotá, Colombia; Cali, Colombia; Caracas, Venezuela; and Panama City, Panama. The company then flew to Mexico City for its final Latin engagement. Opening night at the Teatro Bellas Artes on October 11 was greeted by torrential rain and winds. Though the house was only two-thirds full, the production was enthusiastically greeted. Its popularity was such that it stayed in Mexico for an extra week.

The final European tour began on November 9, 1955, in Antwerp, Belgium, for a return engagement. *Porgy and Bess* then visited Germany for a month, playing in Düsseldorf, where 2,800 people turned out for the opening; Frankfort, Munich, and Berlin, the latter for the second time.

Perhaps the ultimate achievement for the universally appealing *Porgy and Bess* was the trip to Russia and the Iron Curtain countries. One story has it that the invitation to visit Russia was first extended by Andrei Vishinsky when *Porgy and Bess* was playing in New York in 1953. When the State Department was once again approached to underwrite the trip, the decision came back that the trip would be "politically premature." The Russian government then decided to finance the tour. A contract was drawn up on December 3, 1955, providing for the Soviets to pay the management $8,000 weekly in American currency and $8,000 in rubles, as well as all transportation within their boundaries, board and lodging

for a company of 85. The weekly loss sustained by Everyman
Opera was between $4,500 and $5,000 a week for the engagements in Russia, Poland, and Czechoslovakia. In all, the
cost to the Russian government was approximately $150,000.
Though the box-office receipts exceeded this figure by a good
margin, it was not possible for the Soviets actually to turn a
profit. Not only did they have to pay the *Porgy and Bess*
company, but approximately a thousand people attached to
the Stanislavsky Theatre for *not* playing during the time
Porgy and Bess was in Russia. It was planned for the orchestra
from the Stanislavsky Theatre in Moscow to go to Leningrad
and play the engagement there as well.

A great crowd welcomed the company upon its arrival in
Leningrad. The actors were continuously surrounded by
friendly people during their stay. Some attended a Baptist
church on Christmas Day, others broadcast carols, and still
others took over the bandstand at the Astoria Hotel for an
impromptu jam session. After five days of rehearsals with the
Moscow orchestra, the première took place at the Palace of
Culture on December 26, 1955. The top-priced tickets sold for
$15 and the theater was filled to its capacity of 2,200. In
Leningrad they were selling tickets in the so-called black
market for as high as 125 rubles and later in Moscow as high
as 200 rubles. The official rate of exchange is four rubles to a
dollar. Ambassador Bohlen attended, pointedly refuting communist propaganda that the United States government cares
little for the Negro. The interior of the theater was decorated
with the crossed flags of the two countries, and both national
anthems were played. This was the first appearance of an
American acting company inside Russia since the Bolshevik
Revolution. The Russians insisted on having a representative of
the Ministry of Culture read the plot outlines from the stage

before each act. The audiences, though, showed no difference in response to audiences anywhere else in Europe. *Porgy and Bess* never needed any plot outline in the programs for audiences to understand what was going on.

The *Evening Leningrad* termed it "A work stamped with brilliant talent and unusual mastery." The *Smena* called it, "One of the most interesting events of the theatrical season." In all, about 30,000 Russians saw the fourteen performances in the second largest city in the country. Immediately after the company opened, the Russian officials approached the management with the idea of extending the Leningrad engagement for several weeks, and also tripling or quadrupling the number of weeks planned for Moscow. But it was impossible because the company had contracts for subsequent bookings. The idea of visiting other cities was also discussed.

The more sophisticated Moscow audience was even more receptive than the one in Leningrad. With police holding back thousands of people milling around outside the Stanislavsky Theatre, *Porgy and Bess* began its run on January 10, 1956, before a capacity audience of 1,500 which burst into applause thirteen times during the performance. After the curtain the reporter for the New York *Times*, Welles Hangen, wrote, "Some spectators wept; others shouted and stamped their feet, but many were still almost hypnotized by the melodies." *Izvestia* conceded, "Our American guests have shown that original art is understandable for people of all countries." According to Horace Sutton in the *Saturday Review*, "Politically, *Porgy and Bess* is a silent secret weapon. The sight of Negro performers and their white executive staff working and eating side by side has caused Russians to stop and ask for explanation."

Khrushchev attended the *second* performance, a break

with the usual protocol. Even the vice-ministers of culture were amazed, almost stupefied that the members of the Presidium came unannounced. They usually attend, if at all, the final performance. Robert Breen questioned the Minister of Culture about the unusual occurrence. He told him, "He's maybe afraid he couldn't get tickets if he waited."

Back in the United States, the Hearst newspapers backed the visit to Russia, declaring that at last the Russian people could see for themselves that American Negroes do not live in virtual bondage, that as free Americans they have the opportunity to develop their artistic talents. Other newspapers felt that better understanding between peoples of the two countries would develop as a result of this type of cultural visit. Some papers called the *Porgy and Bess* company our ambassadors of good will. The New York *Times* referred to the tour as a "demonstration of true democracy." That Americans can produce great works of art to give the lie to the communist accusation that we are a nation of barbarians was another editorial topic. Everyone agreed that "whenever the best works of American artistic genius are shown to foreign peoples, we are putting our best foot forward," to use the words of the Cincinnati *Enquirer.*

The twelve thousand tickets available for a fifteen-performance run at the Warsaw National Opera House were sold out before the *Porgy and Bess* troupe arrived in town on January 24, 1956. In a city of one million, there had been 500,000 applications for tickets. The opening, attended by the President of Poland and the United States Ambassador, caused the biggest traffic jam since the war, and militiamen had to be stationed on every corner within six blocks of the theater. The press described the ovation as "frantic." "The people came in oxcarts from various parts of Poland," said Ambassador Joseph

Jacobs. "They stood around the streets for nights, even though they knew it was sold out, hoping against hope that they might get in or that a little music might filter out."

Porgy and Bess next played the Wyspianski Theatre in Stalinograd, Poland, then onto the Karlin Theatre in Prague, Czechoslovakia, before returning to Germany for a month. Return engagements were given in Munich and Düsseldorf, in addition to playing Stuttgart and Hamburg. For a final leg of its odyssey, the troupe went to Brussels, Belgium, for the second time, The Hague and Rotterdam in Holland, Oslo, Norway, Aarhus, Denmark, and Amsterdam, Holland. It was here that *Porgy and Bess* completed its travels on June 3, 1956.

To sum up with informal statistics, *Porgy and Bess* played in 29 countries, crossing borders requiring customs inspection 62 times. The audiences spoke 18 different languages! The company was paid in 27 different foreign currencies. During the four years the company was together, with the exception of the 4½ months in London, 10 months in New York, 2½ months in Paris, 6 weeks in Rome, 5 weeks each in Los Angeles and San Francisco, the company moved every week or two to play a total of 70 cities. Of the 208 weeks of the tour, only 31 had been subsidized on three different occasions by ANTA and the State Department. The equipment that was toured for the production weighed between 50,000 and 60,000 pounds. The number in the cast varied from 75 to 90. Of them, it has been said, "Our country has not had a better advertisement than the *Porgy and Bess* troupe—any time, anywhere." *

* NOTE: As this book goes to press, Samuel Goldwyn, perhaps our most distinguished motion-picture producer, is at work on a film version of *Porgy and Bess*, which may well be the climax of its career to date.—M.A.

THEATRE GUILD, 1935

| Boston, Mass. | Colonial Theatre | September 30 (premiere) |
| New York, N. Y. | Alvin Theatre | October 10—124 performances |

THEATRE GUILD TOUR, 1936

Philadelphia, Pa.	Forrest Theatre	January 27–February 8
Pittsburgh, Pa.	Nixon Theatre	February 10–February 15
Chicago, Ill.	Erlanger Theatre	February 17–March 7
Detroit, Mich.	Cass Theatre	March 9–March 14
Washington, D. C.	National Theatre	March 16–March 21

MERLE ARMITAGE PRODUCTIONS, 1938

Pasadena	Municipal Auditorium	February 3
Los Angeles	Philharmonic Auditorium	February 4–February 19
San Francisco	Curran Theatre	February 21–March 8

CHERYL CRAWFORD TOUR, 1942–44

Rochester, N. Y.	Masonic Auditorium	September 28–30, 1942
Buffalo, N. Y.	Erlanger Theatre	October 1–October 3
Cleveland, Ohio	Hanna Theatre	October 5–October 10
Detroit, Mich.	Cass Theatre	October 12–October 24
Cincinnati, Ohio	Taft Auditorium	October 26–October 31

CHERYL CRAWFORD TOUR, 1942–44 (Continued)

City	Theatre	Dates
Chicago, Ill.	Studebaker Theatre	November 2, 1942–January 16, 1943
St. Louis, Mo.	American Theatre	January 18–January 30
Kansas City, Mo.	Municipal Auditorium	February 3–February 6
Minneapolis, Minn.	Lyceum Theatre	February 8–February 11
St. Paul, Minn.	Auditorium	February 12–February 13
Milwaukee, Wis.	Davidson Theatre	February 15–February 20
Detroit, Mich.	Cass Theatre	February 22–February 27 (second visit)
Indianapolis, Ind.	English Theatre	March 2–March 6
Toronto, Canada	Royal Alexander Theatre	March 8–March 13
Pittsburgh, Pa.	Nixon Theatre	March 15–March 27
Philadelphia, Pa.	Forrest Theatre	March 29–April 17
San Francisco, Cal.	Curran Theatre	April 26–May 8
Portland, Ore.	Auditorium	May 25–May 29
Oakland, Cal.	Auditorium	June 9–June 13
Denver, Colo.	Auditorium	June 16–June 19
New York, N. Y.	44th St. Theatre	September 13–October 2, 1943 (24 performances)
Baltimore, Md.	Ford's Theatre	October 4–October 9
Boston, Mass.	Colonial Theatre	October 11–October 23
New Haven, Conn.	Shubert Theatre	October 27–October 30
Springfield, Mass.	Court Sq. Theatre	November 3
Hartford, Conn.	Bushnell Auditorium	November 4–November 6
Williamsport, Pa.	Karlton Theatre	November 10

Harrisburg, Pa.	State Theatre	November 11
Trenton, N. J.	War Memorial Auditorium	November 12–November 13
Greensboro, N. C.	State Theatre	November 17
Raleigh, N. C.	Carolina Theatre	November 18
Columbia, S. C.	Auditorium	November 19
Asheville, N. C.	Plaza Theatre	November 20
Louisville, Ky.	Memorial Auditorium	November 24
Columbus, Ohio	Hartman Theatre	November 25–November 27
St. Louis, Mo.	American Theatre	November 29–December 4 (second visit)
Memphis, Tenn.	Auditorium	December 8
Jackson, Miss.	Auditorium	December 9
Fort Worth, Texas	Auditorium	December 11
Austin, Texas	Paramount Theatre	December 15
San Antonio, Texas	Texas Theatre	December 16–December 17
Dallas, Texas	Auditorium	December 18
Oklahoma City, Okla.	Shrine Auditorium	December 29
Tulsa, Okla.	Convention Hall	December 30–December 31
Dayton, Ohio	Victory Theatre	January 5, 1944
Columbus, Ohio	Hartman Theatre	January 6–January 8 (second visit)
Saginaw, Mich.	Temple Theatre	January 12
Lansing, Mich.	Michigan Theatre	January 13
Grand Rapids, Mich.	Keith Theatre	January 14–January 15

CHERYL CRAWFORD TOUR, 1942–44 (Continued)

Buffalo, N. Y.	Erlanger Theatre	January 17–January 19 (second visit)
Erie, Pa.	Shea Theatre	January 20
Youngstown, Ohio	Park Theatre	January 21–January 22
Cincinnati, Ohio	Taft Auditorium	January 27–January 29 (second visit)
Baltimore, Md.	Ford's Theatre	January 31–February 5 (second visit)
New York, N. Y.	N. Y. City Center	February 7–February 19 (sixteen performances)
Newark, N. J.	Mosque Theatre	February 21–February 26
New York, N. Y.	N. Y. City Center	February 28–April 8 (forty-eight performances)

UNITED STATES TOUR, 1952

Dallas, Texas	State Fair Auditorium	June 9
Chicago, Ill.	Civic Opera House	June 25
Pittsburgh, Pa.	Nixon Theatre	July 22
Washington, D. C.	National Theatre	August 6

EUROPE, 1952–1953

Vienna, Austria	Volksoper	September 7–September 12
Berlin, Germany	Titania Palast	September 18–September 27
London, England	Stoll Theatre	October 9–February 10, 1953
Paris, France	Théâtre de l'Empire	February 16–March 1

NEW YORK, N. Y., 1953

Ziegfeld Theatre   March 10–November 28

UNITED STATES AND CANADA, 1953–54

Philadelphia, Pa.	Forrest Theatre	December 1–December 19
Washington, D. C.	National Theatre	December 21–January 16, 1954
		(second visit)
Richmond, Va.	Mosque Theatre	January 18–January 23
Pittsburgh, Pa.	Nixon Theatre	January 25–January 30
		(second visit)
Cincinnati, Ohio	Taft Theatre	February 1–February 6
St. Louis, Mo.	American Theatre	February 8–February 20
Kansas City, Mo.	Music Hall	February 22–February 28
Chicago, Ill.	Civic Opera House	March 2–March 20
		(second visit)
Minneapolis, Minn.	Lyceum Theatre	March 24–April 3
Toronto, Ontario	Royal Alexandra Theatre	April 6–April 17
Detroit, Mich.	Cass Theatre	April 19–May 8
Cleveland, Ohio	Hanna Theatre	May 10–May 22
Columbus, Ohio	Hartman Theatre	May 24–May 29
Denver, Colo.	Denver Auditorium	June 1–June 5
San Francisco, Cal.	Curran Theatre	June 14–July 10
Los Angeles, Cal.	Philharmonic Auditorium	July 12–August 14

UNITED STATES AND CANADA, 1953–54 (*Continued*)

Boston, Mass.	Shubert Theatre	August 20–August 28
Toronto, Ontario	Royal Alexandra Theatre	August 31–September 11 (second visit)
Montreal, Quebec	Her Majesty's Theatre	September 13–September 18

EUROPE AND MIDDLE EAST, 1954–55

Venice, Italy	Teatro La Fenice	September 22–September 25
Paris, France	Théâtre de l'Empire	September 30–December 4 (second visit)
Zagreb, Yugoslavia	Théâtre de l'Opéra	December 11–December 14
Belgrade, Yugoslavia	Théâtre de l'Opéra	December 16–December 18
Alexandria, Egypt	Théâtre Mohamed Aly	December 31–January 2, 1955
Cairo, Egypt	Théâtre de l'Opéra	January 7–January 12
Athens, Greece	Royal National Theatre	January 17–January 22
Tel Aviv, Israel	Habimah Theatre	January 26–January 30
Casablanca	(concert only)	January 31
Barcelona, Spain	Gran Teatro del Liceo and Windsor Palace	
Naples, Italy	Teatro di San Carlo	February 3–February 13
Milan, Italy	Teatro Alla Scala	February 15–February 17
Genoa, Italy	Teatro Carlo Felice	February 23–February 27
Florence, Italy	Teatro Comunale	March 1–March 6
		March 9–March 13

Lausanne, Switzerland	Théâtre de Beaulieu	March 16–March 23
Marseilles, France	Opéra Municipal	March 26–April 3
Turin, Italy	Teatro Alfieri	April 9–April 13
Rome, Italy	Teatro Quattro Fontane	April 21–May 14
Zurich, Switzerland	Hallenstadion	June 3–June 12
Brussels, Belgium	Théâtre de la Monnaie	June 15–June 21
Antwerp, Belgium	Théâtre de l'Hippodrome	June 23–June 30

LATIN AMERICA, 1955

Rio de Janeiro, Brazil	Teatro Municipal	July 7–July 13
São Paulo, Brazil	Teatro Santana	July 16–July 24
Montevideo, Uruguay	Teatro Solis	July 26–July 31
Buenos Aires, Argentina	Teatro Astral	August 3–August 21
Santiago, Chile	Teatro Municipal	August 25–August 30
Lima, Peru	Teatro Municipal	September 3–September 7
Bogotá, Colombia	Teatro Colombia	September 13–September 18
Cali, Colombia	Teatro Municipal	September 21–September 23
Caracas, Venezuela	Teatro Municipal	September 27–October 3
Panama City, Panama	Teatro Nacional	October 6–October 7
Mexico City, Mexico	Teatro Bellas Artes	October 11–October 25

EUROPE, 1955–1956

Antwerp, Belgium	Théâtre de l'Hippodrome	November 9–November 16 (second visit)
Düsseldorf, Germany	Apollo Theater	November 18–November 22

EUROPE, 1955–56 (Continued)

Frankfort, Germany	Grosses Haus der Städtischen Bühnen	November 25–November 27
Munich, Germany	Deutsches Theatre	December 1–December 6
Berlin, Germany	Titania Palast	December 9–December 15 (second visit)
Leningrad, USSR	Palace of Culture	December 26–January 5, 1956
Moscow, USSR	Stanislavsky Theatre	January 10–January 17
Warsaw, Poland	National Opera House	January 24–February 1
Stalinograd, Poland	Wyspianski Theatre	February 4–February 8
Prague, Czechoslovakia	Karlin Theatre	February 11–February 19
Munich, Germany	Deutsches Theatre	February 22–February 29 (second visit)
Stuttgart, Germany	Staats Theater	March 1–March 4
Hamburg, Germany	Opera House	March 7–March 11
Düsseldorf, Germany	Apollo Theater	March 16–March 22 (second visit)
Brussels, Belgium	Théâtre de la Monnaie	March 25–March 31 (second visit)
The Hague, Holland	Gebouw Voor Kunsten En Wetenschappen	April 2–April 10
Rotterdam, Holland	Luxor Cinema Theatre	April 13–April 20
Oslo, Norway	Volks Theatre	April 25–May 6
Aarhus, Denmark	Aarhushallen	May 9–May 16
Amsterdam, Holland	Theatre Carre	May 19–June 3

Bibliography and Acknowledgments

ARMITAGE, MERLE. *George Gershwin*. New York, Longmans, Green & Co., Inc., 1938.

EWEN, DAVID. *Journey to Greatness*. New York, Henry Holt & Co., Inc., 1956.

EWEN, DAVID. *The Story of George Gershwin*. New York, Henry Holt & Co., Inc., 1943.

GOLDBERG, ISAAC. *George Gershwin*. New York, Simon and Schuster, Inc., 1931.

LEVANT, OSCAR. *A Smattering of Ignorance*. New York, Doubleday & Company, Inc., 1940.

SELDES, GILBERT. *The Seven Lively Arts*. New York, Harper & Brothers, 1924.

For "A Note on the Author," I am much indebted to John Charles Thomas.

The caricatures of George Gershwin and Paul Whiteman are the work of William Auerbach-Levy, used with his generous permission.

The editorial assistance of Isabelle Armitage and Lucie Heymann was invaluable, and is greatly appreciated.

Robert Breen provided me with the translated reviews of *Porgy and Bess* from Europe and South America, of which there are thousands.

The American Society of Composers, Authors, and Publishers,

an organization which was tremendously helpful to George Gershwin in the early days of his career, has answered many inquiries.

In writing the history of *Porgy and Bess* I express thanks for research assistance from Lynn Farnol.

Quotations from Stephen Spender appeared in the article, "Are Critics Too Much with Us?" *The New York Times Book Review*, January 15, 1956. Used by permission of the Editors.

Quotations from Alfred Frankenstein, music and art critic of the San Francisco *Chronicle*, are from *Paul Rosenfeld, Voyager in the Arts*. Used by permission.

Quotations from Jean Cocteau are from *Journals of Jean Cocteau*. Used by permission of Criterion Books, Inc.

Quotations from Arnold Haskell are from *Diaghileff*, by Arnold Haskell. Used by permission of Simon and Schuster, Inc.

Quotations from Paul Rosenfeld are from *Discoveries of a Music Critic*, by Paul Rosenfeld. Used by permission of Harcourt, Brace and Company.

GEORGE GERSHWIN'S CONCERT WORKS

1922
135th Street, originally entitled *Blue Monday.* One-act opera, with libretto by B. G. Sylva. Première: *Scandals of 1922,* the Globe Theatre, August 29, 1922. (One performance.)

1924
Rhapsody in Blue, for piano and orchestra. Paul Whiteman and orchestra, with George Gershwin as soloist. Première: Aeolian Hall, New York, February 12, 1924.

1925
Concerto in F, for piano and orchestra. New York Symphony Society, Walter Damrosch conducting, with George Gershwin as soloist. Première: Carnegie Hall, New York, December 3, 1925.

1926
Three Preludes, for piano only. Première: The composer as soloist, Hotel Roosevelt, New York, November 4, 1926.

1928
An American in Paris, tone poem for orchestra. New York Philharmonic-Symphony Society, Walter Damrosch conducting. Première: Carnegie Hall, New York, December 13, 1928.

"In the Mandarin's Orchid Garden," concert song. Lyrics by Ira Gershwin. Première: Eleanor Marum, Blackstone Theatre, Chicago, November 10, 1929.

1931
Second Rhapsody, for piano and orchestra. Boston Symphony Orchestra, Serge Koussevitzky conducting, with George Gershwin as soloist. Première: Symphony Hall, Boston, January 29, 1932.

1932
Piano transcriptions of eighteen songs, published by Simon and Schuster, 1932. Songs: "Swanee"; "Nobody but You"; "I'll Build a Stairway to Paradise"; "Do It Again"; "Fascinating Rhythm"; "Oh, Lady Be Good"; "Somebody Loves Me"; "Sweet

and Low Down"; "That Certain Feeling"; "The Man I Love"; "Clap Yo' Hands"; "Do, Do, Do"; "My One and Only"; " 'S Wonderful"; "Strike Up the Band"; "Liza"; "I Got Rhythm."

Cuban Overture, for symphony orchestra and Cuban percussion instruments. Lewisohn Stadium Orchestra, Albert Coates conducting. Première: Lewisohn Stadium, New York, August 16, 1932.

1934
Variations on I Got Rhythm, for piano and orchestra. Leo Reisman Orchestra, Charles Previn conducting, with George Gershwin as soloist. Première: Boston, January 14, 1934.

1935
Porgy and Bess, opera in three acts, with libretto by DuBose Heyward. Lyrics by DuBose Heyward and Ira Gershwin. Première: Colonial Theatre, Boston, September 30, 1935.

GEORGE GERSHWIN'S MUSIC IN
STAGE PRODUCTIONS

1918   *Half-Past Eight*
1919   *Capitol Revue*
         La, La, Lucille
         The Morris Gest Midnight Whirl
1920   *Broadway Brevities of 1920*
         The Scandals of 1920
         A Dangerous Maid
1921   *The Scandals of 1921*
1922   *George White's Scandals of 1922*
         Our Nell
1923   *George White's Scandals of 1923*
         The Rainbow Review
1924   *George White's Scandals of 1924*
         Lady, Be Good
         Primrose
         Sweet Little Devil

1925   *Song of the Flame*
       Tell Me More
       Tip-Toes
1926   *Oh, Kay!*
1927   *Funny Face*
1928   *Rosalie*
       Treasure Girl
1929   *Show Girl*
       Strike Up the Band
1930   *Girl Crazy*
1931   *Of Thee I Sing*
1933   *Let 'Em Eat Cake*
       Pardon My English

GEORGE GERSHWIN'S MOTION-PICTURE SCORES

1931   *Delicious*
1937   *Damsel in Distress*
       Shall We Dance?
1938   *The Goldwyn Follies*
1945   *Rhapsody in Blue*
1947   *The Shocking Miss Pilgrim*
1951   *An American in Paris*

MOTION PICTURES ADAPTED FROM GERSHWIN MUSICALS, WITH GEORGE GERSHWIN'S MUSIC

1932   *Girl Crazy*
1940   *Strike Up the Band*
1941   *Lady, Be Good*
1943   *Girl Crazy*

GEORGE GERSHWIN'S GREAT SONGS AND THE ARTISTS WHO INTRODUCED THEM

"A Woman Is a Sometime Thing" (Edward Matthews in *Porgy and Bess*)

"The Babbitt and the Bromide" (Adele Astaire in *Funny Face*)

"Bess, You Is My Woman Now" (Todd Duncan and Anne Brown in *Porgy and Bess*)

"Bidin' My Time" (The Foursome in *Girl Crazy*)

"Boy, What Love Has Done to Me" (Ethel Merman in *Girl Crazy*)

"But Not for Me" (Ginger Rogers and Willie Howard in *Girl Crazy*)

"Clap Yo' Hands" (Betty Cooper and Harlan Dixon in *Oh, Kay!*)

"Do, Do, Do." (Gertrude Lawrence in *Oh, Kay!*)

"Do It Again" (Irene Bordoni in *The French Doll*)

"Embraceable You" (Ginger Rogers and Allen Kearns in *Girl Crazy*)

"Fascinating Rhythm" (Fred and Adele Astaire in *Lady, Be Good*)

"I Got Plenty o' Nuttin'" (Todd Duncan in *Porgy and Bess*)

"I Got Rhythm" (Ethel Merman in *Girl Crazy*)

"I'll Build a Stairway to Paradise" (*Scandals of 1922*)

"It Ain't Necessarily So" (John W. Bubbles in *Porgy and Bess*)

"I've Got a Crush on You" (Gordon Smith and Doris Carson in *Strike Up the Band*)

"Let's Call the Whole Thing Off" (Fred Astaire and Ginger Rogers in *Shall We Dance?*)

"Liza" (Ruby Keeler and Nick Lucas in *Show Girl*)

"Looking for a Boy" (Queenie Smith in *Tip-Toes*)

"Love Is Here to Stay" (Kenny Baker in *The Goldwyn Follies*)

"Love Is Sweeping the Country" (George Murphy and June O'Day in *Of Thee I Sing*)

"Love Walked In" (Kenny Baker in *The Goldwyn Follies*)

"(The) Man I Love" (Originally written for *Lady, Be Good*, and for the first version of *Strike Up the Band*, but not included in either. Adele Astaire introduced it at the tryout of *Lady, Be*

Good in Philadelphia in 1924. Eva Gauthier sang it at her 1925 recital in Derby, Connecticut)

"Mine" (William Gaxton in *Let 'Em Eat Cake*)

"Nobody But You" (Helen Clark, Lorin Baker, and chorus in *La, La Lucille*)

"Of Thee I Sing" (William Gaxton and Lois Moran in *Of Thee I Sing*)

"Oh, Lady Be Good" (Walter Catlett in *Lady, Be Good*)

"Sam and Delilah" (Ethel Merman in *Girl Crazy*)

"So Am I" (Fred and Adele Astaire in *Lady, Be Good*)

"So Are You" (Eddie Foy, Jr., and Kathryn Hereford in *Show Girl*)

"Somebody Loves Me" (Winnie Lightner in *George White's Scandals of 1924*)

"Someone to Watch Over Me" (Gertrude Lawrence in *Oh, Kay!*)

"Soon" (Margaret Schilling in *Strike Up the Band*)

"Strike Up the Band" (Jim Goff and chorus in *Strike Up the Band*)

"Summertime" (Abbie Mitchell in *Porgy and Bess*)

"Swanee" (Production number in *Capitol Theatre Review*, but projected to fame by Al Jolson in *Sinbad*)

"Sweet and Low Down" (Andrew Tombes, Gertrude McDonald, and Amy Revere in *Tip-Toes*)

" 'S Wonderful" (Adele Astaire and Allen Kearns in *Funny Face*)

"That Certain Feeling" (Queenie Smith and Allen Kearns in *Tip-Toes*)

"That Lost Barber-Shop Chord" (Louis Lazarin and the Pan-American Quartet in *Americana*)

"There's a Boat That's Leavin' Soon for New York" (John W. Bubbles in *Porgy and Bess*)

"They Can't Take That Away from Me" (Fred Astaire in *Shall We Dance?*)

"Typical Self-Made American" (Dudley Clements, Jerry Goff, and chorus in *Strike Up the Band*)

"Who Cares?" (William Gaxton and Lois Moran in *Of Thee I Sing*)

"Wintergreen for President" (Ensemble in *Of Thee I Sing*)

A GERSHWIN DISCOGRAPHY

CAPITOL

Capitol FAP-8206 (45 rpm)	Theme from *Rhapsody in Blue* *Three Preludes for Piano*	Leonard Pennario
Capitol P-8343	*American in Paris* *Rhapsody in Blue*	Leonard Pennario and Hollywood Bowl Symphony Orchestra
Capitol T-303	*American in Paris* *Rhapsody in Blue*	Leonard Pennario and Paul Whiteman
Capitol P-8219	*Concerto in F*	Leonard Pennario and Pittsburgh Symphony Orchestra

COLUMBIA

NUMBER	TITLE	ARTIST
CL 721	*Porgy and Bess—A Symphonic Picture*	André Kostelanetz conducting New York Philharmonic
CL 795	*An American in Paris* *Rhapsody in Blue*	André Kostelanetz and Alec Templeton, piano
CL 822	*Girl Crazy*	Mary Martin with Louise Carlyle and Eddie Chappell; Lehman Engel, conducting
CL 922	*Porgy and Bess— Excerpts*	Lawrence Winters, Inez Matthews; Lehman Engel, conducting
CL 1050	*Oh, Kay!*	Barbara Ruick, Jack Cassidy; Lehman Engel, conducting

OSL 162	*Porgy and Bess* Complete	Lawrence Winters, Camilla Williams, Inez Matthews, Avon Long, Warren Coleman, June McMechen, Helen Dowdy, Eddie Matthews; Lehman Engel, conducting
C₂L 1	*Columbia Album of* *George Gershwin*	Percy Faith
CL 700	*Levant Plays* *Gershwin:* *Rhapsody in Blue* *An American in Paris* *Concerto in F*	André Kostelanetz Oscar Levant, piano

RCA VICTOR

Rhapsody in Blue

NUMBER	ARTIST
447-0145	Paul Whiteman and his concert orchestra; George Gershwin, pianist
Album LM-358	Fiedler, Boston Pops Orchestra; Jesus Sanroma, pianist
CAL-135	Raymond Paige and his orchestra
ERA-145 LM-9018	Amparo and José Iturbi, pianists; RCA Victor Symphony Orchestra
LPM-1429 EPA-565	Byron Janis, pianist; Hugo Winterhalter and his orchestra
CAL-304	Jesus Maria Sanroma; Fiedler, Boston Pops
ERA-285 LM-2017 LM-6033	Morton Gould and his orchestra; Morton Gould, pianist
LX-1092 EXA-265	Neal Hefti and his orchestra

An American in Paris

LM-9020	Arturo Toscanini, NBC Symphony Orchestra
LM-2002	Morton Gould and his orchestra
ERA-299	
LM-6033	
LPM-1291	Magic Violins of Villa Fontana
EPB-1291	

Concerto in F

CAL-304	Jesus Maria Sanroma, Boston Pops Orchestra
LPM-1051 EPA-916	The Sauter-Finegan Orchestra
LM-2017	Morton Gould and his orchestra
LM-6033	

Porgy and Bess (selections)

LM-1124	Risë Stevens, Robert Merrill; The Robert Shaw Chorale; RCA-Victor Orchestra
ERA-179	Medley from *Porgy and Bess*; Boston Pops
LM-1879	Orchestra; Fiedler, conductor
LM-2071	
LM-2002	Suite from *Porgy and Bess*; Morton Gould and his orchestra

Preludes

LM-2146	*Prelude No. 2*, Joseph Eger
LM-6033	*Preludes Nos. 2 and 3*, Morton Gould
LM-2017	*Preludes Nos. 1, 2, and 3*, Morton Gould

NOTE: There are multiple recordings of the following:
"Oh, Lady Be Good"; "The Man I Love"; "Love Walked In"; "Summertime"; "I Got Rhymth"; "Somebody Loves Me"; "It Ain't Necessarily So"; "Embraceable You"; "A Foggy Day"; "Bess, You Is My Woman Now"; "Strike Up the Band"; "'S Wonderful"; "Who Cares?"; "Fascinating Rhythm"; "Maybe"; "Do, Do, Do"; "Clap Yo' Hands"; "Bidin' My Time"; "Song of the Flame"; "Nice Work If You Can Get It"; "Wintergreen for President"; "Someone to Watch Over Me"; "I Got Plenty o' Nuttin' "; "Where Is My Bess?"; "Soon."